AN ADULT READING OF BIBLE STORIES

Stories For Personal Reflection And Spiritual Growth.
Reclaim *Your Faith, And* ***Cultivate*** *A Deeper Understanding Of The Living Word.*

Jeanne A. Hawkins

CONTENTS

INTRODUCTION

While sitting alone in my living room one night, a heavy sensation pressed against my chest. Choir practice had wrapped up hours before, yet disquiet lingered. After decades of singing praises of faith, hope, and love, I found myself in profound doubt. The stories of Moses, David, and Esther, which had once imbued me with strength, now felt remote, akin to myths from an alien realm. I questioned their place and significance in our tumultuous, modern existence: "In today's chaotic world, do these ancient narratives still hold value? Are they still relevant?" That night marked the beginning of a journey. It is a journey to find answers for myself and anyone who has ever felt lost or confused about their faith. This book is a testament to that quest. It aims to provide adults with Bible stories that are not only relatable but also transformative. These stories are meant to be a mirror, reflecting our struggles, our triumphs, and our endless search for meaning. They are here to help you reclaim your faith, remove any confusion, and deepen your understanding of the Living Word.

Indeed, my connection to these narratives is profound. Years of participation in a gospel choir have deeply rooted me in the stories and songs that shape our collective spirituality. Yet, this journey was not without its challenges. There were moments when I found myself questioning the very bedrock of my faith. The lyrics that once inspired me frequently sparked more questions than they answered. Particularly in these challenging times, as the world appears increasingly unsettled, seeking clarity and understanding through these age-old texts became a personal crusade.

This book reaches out to those who have matured alongside these stories yet yearn for a more profound comprehension. It extends a hand to the skeptics, the questioners, and those feeling adrift in their spiritual journey. It beckons to all who desire to rediscover their faith, dispel uncertainties, and fully grasp the scriptures. Together, we will revisit 50 biblical narratives with a discerning and thoughtful perspective, drawing parallels between the wisdom of yesteryears and the complexities of our current reality. The distinctiveness of this book lies in its methodology. Instead of merely recounting Bible stories, we delve into their historical and cultural backdrops, examining their relevance to today's world. We engage with thought-provoking questions that provoke deep reflection. This book transcends a straightforward narrative to foster active engagement, reflection, and personal growth. Designed to be approachable, pertinent, and meaningful, each story invites you to connect with its essence.

Each chapter will provide the original text, a modern-day comparison, and questions for personal reflection. We will start with well-known stories like David, Goliath, and the

Prodigal Son. Then, we will move to lesser-known tales that hold equally powerful lessons. The goal is to offer a balanced mix that caters to a wide range of readers.

This book blends ancient wisdom with modern relevance. We won't just read these stories; we will live them. By comparing these stories to current events, we can see how the lessons taught within them apply to our lives today. This approach allows you to determine how your reactions may differ after better understanding the lessons taught within the stories.

So, let's start this journey together. Let's re-read these stories with open hearts and minds. Let's question, reflect, and grow. I invite you to join me in exploring these timeless stories. Let's see how they can illuminate our paths and bring us closer to a more in-depth understanding of the Word.

CHAPTER ONE

UNDERSTANDING THE GENESIS OF FAITH

The Creation narrative was a cornerstone of my youth, often shared by my Sunday School teachers. The story of the Creation was brought to life by the imagery of a divine sculptor shaping the cosmos from nothingness. This tale enchanted me in my youth, feeling more like an enthralling epic than a bedrock of truth. However, as years passed, I delved deeper into the complex layers embedded within these ancient stories. This chapter aims to deepen your understanding of the story of Creation, examining its rich symbolism and theological depth. We will explore how these timeless lessons remain relevant in our contemporary lives.

CREATION REVISITED: INSIGHTS BEYOND THE GARDEN

The story of Creation in Genesis is more than just an account of how the world began. It speaks to deeper truths about our existence and our relationship with God. One of the most profound concepts is the Imago Dei, or Image of

God. According to Genesis 1:26-27, humans are created in God's image, which implies we possess a unique moral and relational likeness to our Creator. This idea elevates our understanding of human dignity, suggesting that every person carries a reflection of the divine. Knowing we share this sacred imprint challenges us to see each other with respect and love.

The Sabbath, as introduced in the Creation narrative, carries profound symbolic significance far beyond the mere cessation of work. On the seventh day, God's rest served not as a pause but as a deliberate act, signifying the completion and sanctification of the created world. This act of resting underscored the work's wholeness and perfection, marking the universe's transition from chaos to order, from formlessness to beauty. In the tapestry of Jewish and Christian traditions, the concept of the Sabbath evolved into a fundamental institution—a time set apart for rest, reflection, and worship. It embodies the principle that rest, akin to work, is sacred and integral to the human experience. The Sabbath reminds us of the rhythm of creation, inviting us to participate in a cycle that alternates between engagement with the world and withdrawal into the sanctuary of rest and spiritual renewal. This divinely ordained pause offers a counterbalance to the relentless pace of modern existence. It challenges the prevailing ethos that equates busyness with importance, urging us to reclaim rest as a divine mandate. Observing a day of rest, in whatever form that may take, allows us to rejuvenate our spirits, reflect on our place in the universe, and deepen our connection with the divine. In this sacred time, we are encouraged to detach from our temporal concerns and immerse ourselves in the eternal, fostering a sense of peace and grounding that nourishes our souls. Thus, the Sabbath is a testament to the inherent value of rest, woven into the fabric of creation from the beginning. It calls us to embrace rest not as an optional luxury but as an essential component of a balanced, spiritually fulfilling life.

Another vital aspect of the Creation story is the notion of stewardship. God entrusted humans with the care of the Earth, calling us to be its stewards. This responsibility involves using resources wisely and protecting and nurturing the environment. Stewardship is a call to balance our needs with the planet's health. It encourages sustainable living and respect for all forms of life.

To truly understand the profound layers of the Creation narrative, it's essential to weave it into the rich mosaic of ancient Near Eastern mythology. The Genesis account shares thematic parallels with myths like the Enuma Elish, where a primordial state of chaos precedes a divine act of creation, ultimately leading to rest. Yet, the Genesis story distinguishes itself by depicting a singular, all-powerful God who brings the universe into being without the turmoil and conflict characteristic of other myths, such as the divine combat seen in the Enuma Elish. This contrast underscores the unparalleled sovereignty and peace inherent in the concept of Israel's God, Yahweh, setting a distinct tone of harmony and purpose in the world's creation.

The Creation story was passed down through generations via oral tradition before being written. This method of storytelling ensured that the narrative was accessible and relatable to the people of ancient Israel. Understanding this context helps us appreciate the rich tapestry of meaning woven into the Genesis account.

In modern times, the Creation story calls us to be responsible stewards of the Earth. Ecological movements inspired by faith emphasize the moral duty to protect our planet. For example, the Evangelical Environmental Network advocates for creation care, urging believers to engage in practices that reduce environmental harm. Practical steps include recycling, conserving water, and supporting sustainable agriculture.

Reflect on what it means to be created in God's image. How does this understanding shape your view of yourself and others? Consider also how you can practice stewardship in your community. Participating in local clean-up efforts or supporting eco-friendly initiatives can significantly impact. By revisiting the Creation story with a mature perspective, we can find profound insights that guide our lives and strengthen our faith.

THE FALL: LESSONS ON HUMAN NATURE AND REDEMPTION

When we think of the story of Adam and Eve, many of us recall a garden, a serpent, and a forbidden fruit. But beneath the surface of this narrative lies a profound exploration of human nature and the concept of original sin. The Tree of Knowledge of Good and Evil, standing in the middle of Eden, symbolizes the boundary set by God. It represents the moral limits given to humanity, a reminder that we are not the ultimate arbiters of right and wrong. Eating the forbidden fruit marks a conscious decision to step beyond those boundaries, highlighting the role of free will. This story is not just about disobedience; it is about the human inclination to seek autonomy, to desire knowledge and power, even at the cost of divine harmony.

The theological implications of the Fall stretch wide and deep, touching the very core of Christian spirituality and understanding of human nature. Central to this is the doctrine of original sin, which posits humanity's inherited sinfulness as a direct consequence of Adam and Eve's defiance in Eden. This seminal event, symbolized by consuming the forbidden fruit from the Tree of Knowledge of Good and Evil, illustrates a singular act of disobedience and a fundamental shift in the human condition. It marks the inception of a profound estrangement between humanity and the divine, a rift that permeates every aspect of human existence. This notion of original sin does more than highlight humanity's penchant for choosing self-interest and autonomy over obedience to God; it reveals an inherent flaw in the fabric of human nature. Yet, paradoxically, a powerful undercurrent of hope exists within this degradation framework.

The narrative of the Fall, while delineating the origins of sin, also sets the stage for the journey toward redemption. It portrays humans as creatures marred by sin but not forsaken, capable of seeking reconciliation and restoration with their Creator. The symbolism of the Tree of Knowledge of Good and Evil is pivotal in this narrative, serving as a metaphor for the boundary between divine wisdom and human curiosity, between sanctioned obedience and forbidden autonomy. The act of transgressing this boundary is emblematic of humanity's inherent desire to transcend its limitations, to reach beyond the prescribed into the realm of the divine. This act of reaching beyond precipitates the Fall and encapsulates the dual nature of human existence: flawed and finite, yet imbued with the capacity for spiritual redemption. In this light, the story of the Fall is not merely a tale of temptation and transgression but a profound exploration of human nature itself. It confronts the reality of our imperfections and invites us to contemplate the possibility of redemption through grace. Understanding the depth and nuance of this narrative enables us to grasp the complexity of our relationship with the divine, marked by frailty and the potential for renewal and grace.

Exploring its historical and cultural roots is imperative to appreciate the story's profound message fully. The Genesis narrative shares thematic threads with ancient Near Eastern mythology, notably the Mesopotamian tale of Adapa. In this story, Adapa, granted immense wisdom by the God Ea, encounters a forbidden act that ultimately costs him the gift of immortality. This motif of a forbidden act leading to grave consequences mirrors the pivotal moment in the Genesis account where a similar transgression seals humanity's fate. The serpent, a central figure in The Fall, carries layers of symbolism that vary widely across ancient cultures, enriching the narrative's complexity. In Mesopotamian mythology, the serpent is often seen as an emblem of wisdom and immortality, attributes that add depth to its role in Genesis. Rather than a mere deceiver, the serpent represents a multifaceted symbol of knowledge and the duality of life's essence—offering enlightenment at the cost of innocence. This more nuanced view of the serpent in Genesis encourages readers to delve deeper into the story's implications. By noting similarities with tales like that of Adapa, we see how Genesis weaves itself into a broader fabric of mythological traditions that confront themes of knowledge, temptation, and the repercussions of our choices. This broader context enriches our understanding of the serpent's role, showing it not merely as the trigger for humanity's Fall but as a central figure in our ongoing journey toward understanding, highlighting the risks that this journey inevitably brings.

The expansive narrative of Genesis situates the Fall amidst the tapestry of human history and divine encounters. It lays the groundwork for the evolving saga of humanity's bond with God, accentuated by themes of covenant and salvation. Grasping these cultural and historical contexts deepens our comprehension, revealing how the ancient Israelites employed well-known symbols and narratives to articulate distinct theological truths.

Connecting the Fall to contemporary issues of morality and ethics reveals its enduring relevance. In today's world, the temptation is as accurate as ever. Whether it's the lure of power, wealth, or forbidden pleasures, we face choices that test our moral boundaries. The Fall teaches us about the consequences of yielding to temptation and the importance of personal accountability. By examining Adam and Eve's actions, we can reflect on our decisions and moral dilemmas.

Personal accountability is crucial in navigating these dilemmas. The story of the Fall reminds us that our choices have repercussions for ourselves and others. In a society where blame-shifting is common, taking responsibility for our actions is a powerful act of integrity. It opens the door to redemption, allowing us to seek forgiveness and make amends.

Reflect on how you deal with temptation in your life. What strategies do you use to resist it, and where do you find strength? Consider also the steps you can take to seek redemption in your relationships. Whether apologizing for a wrong or making a positive change, redemption is about restoring harmony and trust. The story of the Fall encourages us to look inward, to understand our flaws, and to strive for a better, more harmonious relationship with ourselves, others, and the divine.

CAIN AND ABEL: UNDERSTANDING JEALOUSY AND FORGIVENESS

Many of us have heard the story of Cain and Abel growing up, but its depth often eludes us. At its core, this story is about the destructive power of jealousy and the redemptive potential of forgiveness. Cain and Abel, Adam and Eve's first children, brought offerings to God. Abel's offering, a choice portion of his flock, pleased God, while Cain's offering of fruits from the ground did not. This distinction in their offerings touches on more than just material gifts; it delves into the intentions behind them. Abel's offering was given with a heart full of faith and reverence, while Cain's lacked that same spirit. The significance of these offerings reveals how our inner dispositions shape our actions and their outcomes.

Cain's growing jealousy towards Abel, fueled by the perceived preferential treatment from God, spiraled into an irreversible tragedy. While Abel's offerings found favor with

God, Cain's did not, igniting a flame of envy that would ultimately consume him. Unable to quell the rising tide of resentment, Cain orchestrated a moment of betrayal that would forever alter the course of humanity. He deceitfully led Abel into the solitude of a field, where he committed the first act of fratricide recorded in biblical history. This harrowing incident underscores the profound consequences of unchecked jealousy, illustrating how such a corrosive emotion can dismantle the very fabric of familial bonds and lead to irrevocable acts of violence.

The narrative of Cain and Abel serves as a mirror reflecting the complex interplay of emotions, ethics, and divine interaction that shaped the beliefs and values of ancient societies. This tale, emblematic of the destructive power of jealousy and the profound consequences of moral failure, resonates with the universal theme of sibling rivalry. This motif transcends cultural and temporal boundaries. The stark outcome of Cain's actions—a life marred by exile and divine retribution—is a cautionary tale about allowing envy to fester unaddressed. Moreover, this story accentuates the importance of self-mastery and the need for individuals to govern their darkest impulses.

In its recounting, we are prompted to reflect on our responses to perceived injustices and how we navigate our most challenging emotions. The biblical account of Cain and Abel invites a deep introspection into the human condition, urging us to consider how we might act differently when faced with similar feelings of rejection or inadequacy. In the broader cultural and historical context, the story of Cain and Abel encapsulates themes central to the ancient Near Eastern ethos—such as divine favor, sacrifice, and the moral obligations within family dynamics. These narratives served as moral compasses and reflections of their time's societal norms and spiritual understandings.

Through the prism of this story, ancient cultures could explore and impart lessons on the gravity of moral choices, the sanctity of life, and the pivotal role of divine guidance in human affairs. With its deep emotional and ethical layers, the tale of Cain and Abel continues to offer profound insights into the nature of human relationships, the struggle between right and wrong, and the pursuit of divine favor. It beckons us to confront our shadows, question the roots of our envy and resentment, and seek reconciliation and healing with our fellow beings and the divine.

Sibling rivalry was a common theme in ancient cultures, often symbolizing more significant societal conflicts. In ancient Israelite religion, sacrifices were a critical aspect of worship, representing devotion and obedience to God. The story underscores the importance of offering our best to God materially, spiritually, and emotionally. Understanding this context helps us see the broader implications of Cain's and Abel's actions within their culture and our lives.

Drawing parallels to modern interpersonal relationships, we can see how the story of Cain and Abel offers timeless insights into dealing with jealousy and conflict. Consider the sibling rivalries we observe today. Whether it's the classic tale of two brothers vying for their parent's attention or colleagues competing for a promotion, jealousy can creep in and wreak havoc. In such situations, forgiveness becomes crucial. Practicing forgiveness allows us to release jealousy and resentment's hold on us. It's not about condoning harmful actions but freeing ourselves from the emotional burden they create.

In personal relationships, strategies for practicing forgiveness can vary. One practical approach is open communication. Expressing feelings honestly and listening to the other person's perspective can pave the way for understanding and reconciliation. Another strategy is empathy. Seeing the situation from the other person's viewpoint can soften our hearts and make forgiveness more attainable. For instance, if you've ever felt jealous of a sibling's achievements, consider what it took for them to reach those milestones. This perspective can transform jealousy into admiration and respect.

Reflect on your own experiences with jealousy and forgiveness. Have you ever felt jealous of someone close to you? How did you handle it? Perhaps you distanced yourself or, conversely, confronted the issue head-on. Think about what worked and what didn't. What steps can you take to forgive someone who has wronged you? Maybe it involves a heartfelt conversation, or perhaps it's an internal process of letting go. The story of Cain and Abel encourages us to examine these emotions and actions, pushing us toward healing and growth.

NOAH'S ARK: FAITH AMID DOUBT

In a world overwhelmed by corruption and disbelief, Noah stands as a beacon of unwavering faith and obedience. Imagine being Noah, receiving a divine command to build an enormous ark despite the ridicule and skepticism of those around you. Noah didn't just follow God's instructions; he did so with meticulous detail and steadfast commitment. His faith wasn't fleeting but deeply rooted, guiding him to act against the prevailing tide of moral decay.

As Genesis describes, the Ark is not merely a large boat constructed of gopher wood; it embodies a profound symbol of divine refuge and salvation amidst a world submerged in moral decay. This immense vessel, meticulously crafted according to divine specifications, stands as a beacon of sanctuary amid chaos, a tangible sign of God's mercy where human and animal life could be safeguarded and given a chance for a fresh beginning in a cleansed world. The narrative elevates the Ark from a simple means of survival to a testament of unwavering faith in God's promise and human obedience to divine command. Moreover, the flood's aftermath introduces a pivotal moment in the biblical account—establishing a covenant between God and Noah, representing all of humanity and the living creatures that shared the Ark's refuge.

This covenant, signified by the appearance of a rainbow in the sky, is not just a pledge by God to refrain from destroying the Earth again by flood. It is a symbol laden with the promise of hope, renewal, and God's unwavering fidelity to His creation. This rainbow, with its spectrum of colors arching across the skies after the Great Flood, serves as a celestial reminder of God's grace and His eternal commitment to sustain and nurture life on Earth.

Through this divine assurance, the narrative of Noah's Ark transcends the historical. It enters the realm of the eternal, offering a message that resonates with the themes of redemption and restoration. It reassures us of the Creator's love and protection, reminding us that even in the darkest times, a covenant of salvation embraces humanity and the entirety of the natural world. This covenant, therefore, becomes a cornerstone of faith, a source of spiritual solace, and a call to stewardship towards the Earth and all its inhabitants, echoing through generations as a testament to the enduring bond between the divine and the created order.

Placing the full significance of Noah's Ark within the broader context of ancient flood myths is essential. The Epic of Gilgamesh, one of the oldest-known stories, also features a great flood. In this tale, Utnapishtim builds a boat to save his family and animals from a deluge sent by capricious gods. While there are similarities, such as preserving life through a flood, the differences are striking. In Genesis, the flood is not a result of divine whim but a moral response to human wickedness.

Moreover, the biblical narrative emphasizes a single, just God who establishes a covenant with humanity. This contrasts sharply with the multiplicity of gods in the Gilgamesh epic, mired in their conflicts and whims. These distinctions highlight the unique theological perspective of the Genesis account.

Flood narratives pervade the mythologies of ancient civilizations, serving as archetypal symbols of divine retribution and regeneration. These stories often emerge from a primal human need to make sense of cataclysmic natural events and their ethical ramifications. Within this universal framework, the biblical account of Noah's Ark stands out for its distinctive emphasis on faith, obedience to divine will, and receiving God's mercy. Unlike other ancient flood narratives that might attribute such cataclysms to the caprices of multiple deities, the story of Noah's Ark roots the flood in a moral context, presenting it as a deliberate act by a singular just God to cleanse the world of its corruption and wickedness.

This narrative does not merely recount the survival of Noah and his family; it underscores the resilience of the human spirit, capable of unwavering faith in the face of existential threats. Noah's obedience to God's command, building an ark to save his family and pairs of all living creatures, becomes a testament to his faith and righteousness amidst a morally bankrupt world.

The account of Noah and the Ark transcends a simple tale of survival; it evolves into a profound narrative about the potential for new beginnings, even when faced with seemingly insurmountable devastation. It invites readers to reflect on their capacity for faith and obedience, encouraging a belief in the possibility of redemption and the promise of a fresh start grounded in a divine assurance of protection and fidelity. This story, therefore, not only provides a moral and spiritual compass but also offers a beacon of hope for humanity's capacity for renewal in the face of overwhelming challenges.

Noah's story of unwavering faith offers powerful lessons for us today. Maintaining faith can be incredibly challenging in times of doubt and difficulty. Yet, our faith can become a source of strength and resilience during these moments. Modern-day "arks" or refuges of faith can take various forms, from community support groups to personal spiritual practices. These sanctuaries provide a space for renewal and growth, much like Noah's Ark did in ancient times.

Nurturing faith amid uncertainty requires actionable measures. Integrating oneself into communities that uplift and support, dedicating time to prayer or meditation, and delving deeply into religious texts can bolster our spiritual resilience. Reflecting on instances where faith has been a beacon during tumultuous periods allows us to amass a well-spring of trust and optimism. This accumulated assurance is a steadfast anchor when navigating life's inevitable trials.

Reflect on your own experiences with faith and doubt. When have you felt called to act in faith despite uncertainty? Consider the steps you took and the outcome of those actions. Additionally, think about what kind of "ark" or refuge of faith you can create. This could be a physical space for quiet reflection, a group of like-minded individuals for mutual support, or a personal practice that strengthens your spiritual connection.

The narrative of Noah is not merely a story from the past; it is a vivid illustration of faith's resilience. Amidst adversity, Noah's unwavering belief in the divine serves as a beacon, illuminating the path toward spiritual shelter and rejuvenation. As we face our trials and tribulations, we may draw inspiration from Noah's steadfastness. Let his legacy encourage us to uphold our faith, constructing sanctuaries of hope and fortitude within our hearts and communities.

CHAPTER TWO

PATRIARCHS AND PROMISES

Imagine that you've been living in a place your entire life, surrounded by family and familiar faces. One day, you hear an unmistakable voice telling you to pack up and leave everything behind. There is no clear destination, just a promise of something better. Would you go? This was Abraham's reality when God called him to leave his homeland and journey to an unknown land. It sounds daunting, doesn't it? But Abraham's story is one of unwavering faith, even when the path ahead seemed uncertain.

ABRAHAM'S JOURNEY: TRUSTING GOD'S PROMISES

Abraham's faith journey began with a monumental call to leave his homeland, as recorded in Genesis 12:1-4. Imagine the comfort and security of your hometown, and then imagine being asked to leave it all behind on a promise. God told Abraham, "Go from your country, your people, and your father's household to the land I will show you." Abraham obeyed without hesitation, taking his wife Sarah, his nephew

Lot, and all their possessions. This act of faith set the stage for Abraham's entire life, a journey marked by trust in God's promises despite numerous challenges.

One of God's most significant promises to Abraham was that of numerous descendants, as highlighted in Genesis 15:5-6. God took Abraham outside and said, "Look up at the sky and count the stars—if indeed you can count them. So shall your offspring be." This promise was made when Abraham and Sarah were childless and advanced in years. It must have seemed impossible, yet Abraham believed in God. He counted this belief as righteousness, showing that faith often requires us to trust beyond what we see or understand.

Perhaps the most harrowing test of Abraham's faith unfolded with God's command to sacrifice his son, Isaac, as recounted in Genesis 22:1-12. The narrative reaches a climax when, after years of barrenness and longing, Abraham and Sarah's hopes finally materialize through Isaac's birth. Yet, in a divine test of loyalty and trust, God calls upon Abraham to surrender his long-awaited son as a burnt offering on the desolate heights of Mount Moriah. Faced with a command that threatens the very promise of his lineage, Abraham responds with a resolve that transcends human understanding. He prepares to fulfill God's will with a heart laden with anguish yet steadfast in faith. The journey to Moriah becomes a physical trek and a profound spiritual odyssey into the depths of unwavering faith. Abraham's actions, driven by an unshakeable trust in God's righteousness, illustrate a surrender to divine will unparalleled in human history. As Abraham raises the knife, poised to sacrifice his son, the angel of the Lord intervenes, halting his hand. God provides a ram as a substitute offering in the thicket, sparing

Isaac's life. This moment of divine intervention is a powerful testament to Abraham's unyielding faith that did not falter even when faced with the incomprehensible demand of sacrificing his son. It reveals a profound truth about the nature of divine testing, not as a cruel whim but as a pathway to deeper trust and obedience.

This episode highlights the depth of Abraham's faith and God's faithfulness and provision. The ram caught in the thicket symbolizes God's provision, a testament to the belief that God will provide even in our most desperate moments. This dramatic unfolding on Mount Moriah is a testament to the complex interplay of faith, obedience, and divine provision, inviting readers to contemplate the extent of their trust in divine promises amidst life's most challenging trials.

To fully appreciate Abraham's journey, it's essential to understand the historical and cultural context of ancient Mesopotamia. In that era, the significance of land and kinship was paramount. Land was not just a place to live; it was a source of identity and security. Leaving one's homeland meant severing ties with one's community and heritage, a daunting prospect in ancient societies. Moreover, covenants played a crucial role in ancient Near Eastern cultures. These were solemn agreements, often sealed with rituals, binding the parties involved to their promises. God's covenant with Abraham, promising him land and descendants, was a radical departure from the polytheistic beliefs of his society. Abraham's acceptance of monotheism and trust in God's promises marked a significant shift in religious thought.

In contemporary contexts, Abraham's journey strikingly mirrors the challenges we encounter around trust and obedience in our personal and spiritual lives. The concept of "leaps of faith" is not foreign, manifesting in decisions like career shifts, relocations, or other pivotal life changes. These instances call upon us to trust a higher power, believing in the unseen and the unknown. Abraham's story is a compelling parallel, illustrating the timeless struggle to maintain faith amidst life's uncertainties. It reminds us that, like Abraham, we are often prompted to step into the unknown, supported by the belief in a divine plan that guides our steps, even when the destination remains obscured.

Reflect on the promises of God you are holding onto in your life. Are there areas where you feel called to step out in faith but are hesitant because of uncertainty? Consider how you can demonstrate trust and obedience in your current circumstances. It might involve taking risks, making difficult decisions, or simply waiting patiently for God's timing. Whatever your situation, remember that faith is not just about believing in God's promises but acting on them, even when the path ahead is unclear.

SARAH'S LAUGHTER: FAITH AMIDST DOUBT

Envision receiving news at the age of ninety that you're about to become a parent. Such a declaration might sound utterly preposterous, and indeed, Sarah found it so, responding with laughter. The arrival of three visitors who foretold that Sarah would conceive a son within the year prompted an incredulous chuckle from her, as recorded in

Genesis 18:10-12. This moment of mirth wasn't merely about doubt; it encapsulated years of deferred hopes and the arduous journey of sustaining belief in a promise that appeared increasingly improbable. For Sarah, the notion that she could bear a child at her age seemed more like a mocking jest than a divine pledge. Yet, the unfolding of events would reveal that the Almighty's plans surpass the bounds of human constraints, transforming Sarah's skeptical laughter into a joyous celebration of the miraculous.

The arrival of Isaac, aptly named to mean "laughter," marked the realization of a divine assurance to Sarah and Abraham. Chronicled in Genesis 21:1-7, this extraordinary event underscores the fidelity of God's promises. Initially, Sarah's laughter sprang from skepticism, yet it blossomed into profound joy and wonder upon embracing her son. She joyfully declared, "God has brought me laughter, and everyone who hears of this will share in my joy" (Genesis 21:6). This transition from incredulity to jubilation wasn't solely a personal triumph but a powerful affirmation of God's unwavering loyalty. It illustrated that amidst skepticism and despair, the promises of the divine steadfastly hold to be true. Sarah's passage from doubt to realization is a poignant reminder that faith often entails periods of anticipation and uncertainty. Yet the fruition of God's promises is invariably rewarding.

In the tapestry of ancient Israelite society, the role of childbearing was woven with threads of profound significance. It transcended the mere continuation of the family line, embodying vital aspects of survival, legacy, and social standing. Within this cultural framework, a woman's value was intricately linked to her fertility. The ability to bear children was not just a private hope but a public expectation, with barrenness casting a long shadow of stigma and disenfranchisement. `

Sarah's story is emblematic of the burdensome weight carried by women of her era. The societal lens through which women were viewed magnified their reproductive role, often overshadowing their individual worth. Sarah's barren years were a personal trial and a public spectacle of perceived failure. Her struggle reflects a broader societal construct where women's identities were predominantly defined by their ability to contribute to the lineage. This cultural backdrop rendered Sarah's eventual transition into motherhood a personal victory and a profound transformation of her societal and self-identity.

The psychological and social dimensions of barrenness in such a context cannot be overstated. Women grappling with infertility faced an onslaught of emotional turmoil, compounded by the societal implications of their condition. Her decision to give her maidservant, Hagar, to Abraham as a surrogate mother was a desperate attempt to fulfill the promise through human means. This act, while culturally acceptable, led to further complications and emotional turmoil.

Sarah's story reflects the broader struggles of women in her society, caught between cultural expectations and personal desires. Sarah's journey through this landscape of despair to the pinnacle of motherhood embodies a poignant narrative of resilience. It underscores the emotional and societal resurgence that can follow the fulfillment of a long-awaited promise, highlighting the deep interplay between personal faith and societal expectations. In this light, Sarah's story is a tale of individual triumph and a commentary on the shifting sands of societal norms and personal identity. It invites readers to reflect on the transformative power of faith and perseverance in the face of societal pressures and personal challenges.

From Sarah's experience, we learn valuable lessons about faith amidst doubt. It's easy to become impatient and take matters into our own hands when promises seem delayed. But Sarah's story teaches us the importance of patience and perseverance. Even when it looks like nothing is happening, God is at work behind the scenes. Her journey from doubt to fulfillment encourages us to hold onto our faith, even when circumstances suggest otherwise. Overcoming societal pressures and personal insecurities is a challenge many of us face. Sarah's story reminds us that our worth is not defined by societal standards but by divine promises.

In your journey of faith, encountering doubt is a shared experience. Have you ever found yourself echoing Sarah's laughter, where promises from the divine felt too grand to be real? Such moments of skepticism aren't just challenges; they are invitations to deepen your faith. Doubt and faith are intertwined, encouraging us to seek a more profound comprehension of the divine. Embracing this journey means staying open to the wonders of the sacred, even when they seem unbelievable.

ISAAC AND REBEKAH: LOVE AND DIVINE PROVIDENCE

Consider the profound act of entrusting the search for a life partner for your offspring to the hands of providence. Abraham's decision to find a spouse for Isaac through divine guidance epitomizes faith in action. Entrusting his servant with this critical mission, the servant's approach was steeped in prayer, seeking a sign from God to identify the right woman. This sign was specific: the woman who would not only offer water to him but also to his camels. This woman would be the one chosen for Issac.

The account, detailed in Genesis 24:12-21, unfolds with Rebekah's arrival at the well, where she does precisely as Abraham's servant had prayed for, thereby exhibiting her kindness and role as the fulfillment of a divine orchestration. Her gesture surpassed mere hospitality; it was the physical manifestation of God's guidance and answer to prayer.

Rebekah's decision to depart with the servant, forsaking her family and homeland, underscores her deep faith and reliance on divine guidance. As depicted in Genesis 24:58-61, Rebekah's response, "I will go," was not uttered without considerable thought. In the context of her era, such a move entailed more than physical relocation; it meant severing the deep ties of kinship and security that were foundational to one's identity. Her bold step into the unknown, accepting her destiny as Isaac's spouse, not only reveals her remarkable character and spiritual strength but also signifies her unwavering belief in the divine blueprint for her life.

Delving deeper into the customs and societal norms surrounding marriage in ancient Israelite society, we uncover layers of complexity that enrich our understanding of Isaac and Rebekah's union. In this era, marriages were meticulously arranged, serving not merely as a bond between two individuals but as a strategic alliance between families, intertwining their destinies and resources. The objective was to ensure social cohesion and fortify economic stability across generations. The marriage negotiation was a ceremonial process steeped in tradition and laden with symbolic gestures. Dowries and bridal gifts, pivotal to these negotiations, were far from mere formalities. They represented a tangible expression of alliance and mutual respect between the families involved. These gifts were laden with meaning, symbolizing the transfer of wealth and the establishment of enduring familial bonds. They were a testament to the value placed on marriage as a covenant between the couple and their extended families.

Thus, the intricate dance of marriage negotiations in ancient times, marked by the exchange of dowries and gifts, was critical in forging family alliances. It solidified bonds that were pivotal for the couple's future and their communities' social and economic fabric. In this light, Rebekah's story is a vivid tableau of the socio-cultural and religious tapestries that shaped her journey into Isaac's life, illuminating the profound significance of marriage in ancient Israelite society.

The story of Isaac and Rebekah offers timeless insights into modern relationships and the importance of trusting divine guidance. Many of us can relate to the idea of "divine appointments" in our own lives when we meet someone in a seemingly coincidental yet profoundly meaningful way. Whether it's meeting a future spouse, a mentor, or a lifelong friend, these encounters often feel orchestrated by a higher power. Trusting in divine guidance, as seen in Isaac and Rebekah's union, encourages us to remain open to life's possibilities, even when they come with uncertainties.

Selecting a life partner is one of life's paramount choices, deeply intertwined with faith's guiding hand. The narrative of Isaac and Rebekah underscores trust and faith as foundational pillars in making such pivotal life decisions. It advocates for a belief in a divine blueprint for our lives, assuring us that divine wisdom will lead us to our intended partners. This conviction requires more than mere passivity; it demands active engagement through prayer, discernment, and, at times, bold steps of faith, mirroring Rebekah's courageous departure from her familiar world.

Reflect on how you seek God's guidance in your relationships. Do you pray for direction and signs or rely solely on your judgment? Consider the qualities you value in a life partner and how they align with your faith. Are you seeking someone who shares your values, beliefs, and commitment to spiritual growth? Take a moment to write down these qualities and reflect on how they have influenced your past and present relationships. This exercise can provide clarity and focus as you seek divine guidance in your relational decisions.

The story of Isaac and Rebekah is a testament to the beauty of divine providence, the importance of faith in relationships, and the willingness to trust in God's plan, even when it leads us into the unknown.

JACOB'S LADDER: DREAMS AND DIVINE ENCOUNTERS

Envision yourself in Jacob's shoes: Alone and vulnerable, with nothing but the hard earth beneath you and a stone as your makeshift pillow. While fleeing from your brother Esau's fury, sleep overtakes you, and you're thrust into a vivid vision. A grand ladder connecting the earthly realm to the heavenly, with angels traversing it in both directions, captures your gaze. At its peak, the presence of the Lord looms, extending promises of protection and prosperity. This scene from Genesis 28:12-13 isn't just a fleeting dream; it's a pivotal spiritual encounter. The ladder, bridging the gap between the divine and the mortal, reassures Jacob of God's unwavering support and the enduring promise of a fruitful lineage for his descendants. This vision transcends mere imagery, symbolizing a profound moment of divine affirmation and guidance, a cornerstone in the unfolding narrative of Jacob's destiny and the legacy of his lineage.

In the tapestry of the ancient world, dreams were revered as sacred channels of divine communication. Far from being disregarded as ephemeral flights of fancy, they were considered profound messages imbued with the divine will. This belief permeated ancient Israelite culture, where dreams were idolized as a vital conduit for divine revelation. The narrative of Jacob's dream, with its celestial ladder, is a quintessential illustration of this belief, highlighting the dream as a pivotal moment of divine affirmation and guidance. This tradition of divine dreams was not exclusive to Jacob.

The biblical canon is replete with instances where dreams serve as the divine medium of choice for imparting pivotal revelations. Joseph, with his prophetic dreams, is a prime example. His initial dreams of sheaves and celestial bodies bowing to him not only foreshadowed his eventual ascendancy over his brothers but also hinted at the broader destiny of his family within the divine schema (Genesis 37). Similarly, Daniel's dreams, rich with symbolic imagery, unveiled the succession of empires and divine judgments, laying bare the divine orchestration of human history (Daniel 7-8). These narratives underscore dreams' integral role in shaping the destinies of individuals and nations alike, emphasizing the significance of heeding these nocturnal divine encounters.

The ancient Israelites' engagement with dreams as divine messages underscores a broader theological motif: the active, personal involvement of the sacred in the human saga. Dreams transcended mere information transmission; they were interactive dialogues marked by personal reassurance, prophetic guidance, and, at times, calls to action.

Jacob's dream reaffirmed the Abrahamic covenant; it was a pivotal moment in his journey, enriching his understanding of his unique role in God's ongoing story. This moment in the biblical narrative challenges us to rethink our approach to spiritual communication. In a society that may overlook the mystical, these ancient stories invite us to embrace a broader openness to how God may reach out to us. Dreams, serendipitous occurrences, or even the subtle nudging of our spirit might all be channels of divine insight, offering direction, comfort, and the opportunity for profound change. As we delve into these timeless tales, we are prompted to stay receptive to the divine's subtle guidance, ready to navigate the complexities of life with an awareness of the sacred presence guiding our journey.

Jacob's vision reaffirmed the blessings given to his ancestors, Abraham and Isaac. It served as a cornerstone in the biblical story. The verses of Genesis 28:14-15 reinforce God's covenant: Jacob's descendants would multiply extensively, inhabit vast lands, and become a source of blessing for all the earth's families. This vision went beyond providing mere comfort; it highlighted the unfolding of God's grand plan across generations. For Jacob, this dream was a profound awakening, transforming his view of his role in this divine legacy and reinvigorating his commitment to God's promises.

Such spiritual encounters, exemplified by Jacob's ladder, offer timeless insights for believers today. They invite us to be open to spiritual guidance and the significant impact of mystical experiences. In our fast-paced world, we might overlook dreams and meaningful spiritual moments as trivial or imaginary. However, an openness to engaging with the divine can lead to significant personal growth and spiritual enlightenment. Experiences manifested in dreams, prayer, or moments of deep reflection can change our perspectives, renew our faith, and guide our paths in life.

Reflect on your own life. Have you ever experienced a "divine encounter" that left a lasting impact? Maybe it was a dream, a moment of clarity during prayer, or an unexpected event that felt like a message from above. How did it change you? These encounters, like Jacob's ladder, remind us of the divine connection in our lives. Consider the steps you might take to be more open to God's guidance in your daily life. This might involve setting aside time for quiet reflection, keeping a journal of your dreams and spiritual experiences, or simply remaining open and attentive to the signs and messages that come your way.

Jacob's ladder was more than just a dream; it was a divine encounter that reaffirmed God's promises and transformed Jacob's understanding of his place in God's plan. In our own lives, being open to such encounters can lead to profound personal growth and a deeper connection with the divine. Reflect on your spiritual experiences, remain open to divine guidance, and embrace the transformative power of these encounters.

CHAPTER THREE
EXODUS AND LIBERATION

You are standing alone in the vast expanse of the wilderness, your solitude broken only by the soft sounds of your flock grazing nearby. Suddenly, a bush bursts into flames, yet remarkably, it is not consumed. This extraordinary occurrence marked a pivotal moment in Moses' life as he found himself on Mount Horeb. Compelled by a force beyond his understanding, Moses ventured closer to the bush. To Moses' amazement, a voice echoed from the flames—a voice that shattered the wilderness's quiet, calling "Moses, Moses!" God's voice cut through the mundane to reveal a moment of deep spiritual significance. This was no mere blaze; it represented a theophany, a clear and decisive indication of God's presence among us. This divine encounter did more than summon Moses to a daunting mission, exposing his vulnerabilities—it was poised to reshape his fate and the trajectory of the entire nation of Israel.

MOSES' CALLING: OVERCOMING SELF-DOUBT

Moses' initial reaction to his divine commission was anything but assured. Wrapped in a cloak of hesitation, he doubted his capability to undertake the monumental task of leading the Israelites to freedom. Despite being chosen by God, Moses was blinded by his perceived inadequacies. His extraordinary encounter at the burning bush, as detailed in Exodus 3:1-6, was a moment of profound divine disclosure. In this encounter, God revealed Himself as "I AM WHO I AM," declaring His timeless might and unwavering essence. Moses found himself on consecrated ground, a notion first introduced here, highlighting the sacred disparity between the divine and the mortal.

Nevertheless, in the face of this staggering revelation, Moses was besieged by self-doubt. Moses' reluctance is evident in his excuses. He questioned his worthiness, saying, "Who am I that I should go to Pharaoh and bring the Israelites out of Egypt?" (Exodus 3:11). His feelings of inadequacy were compounded by his fear of being rejected by the Israelites and Pharaoh alike.

Even after God reassured him, Moses continued to express doubt, particularly about his speaking abilities. In Exodus 4:10-12, Moses pleaded, "Pardon your servant, Lord. I have never been eloquent... I am slow of speech and tongue." God's response was straightforward and powerful: "Who gave human beings their mouths? ... Now go; I will help you speak and will teach you what to say." Despite these reassurances, Moses' self-doubt persisted, begging God to send someone else.

The reassurances God offered Moses transcended mere words of comfort. They were substantiated by unequivocal signs that underscored His divine authority and presence.

In the narrative found in Exodus 4:1-8, God furnished Moses with miraculous demonstrations: a staff transforming into a serpent and Moses' hand turning leprous before being restored —each sign a testament to the divine power backing Moses' mission. Furthermore, God provided a solution that underscored His understanding and support, anticipating Moses' apprehensions regarding his oratory skills and recognizing Moses' apprehension, especially concerning his eloquence; God appointed Aaron, Moses' brother, as a spokesman (Exodus 4:14-16). Aaron, known for his articulate speech, was to be Moses' voice, effectively complementing Moses' strengths with his own. This divine intervention demonstrates a profound principle: God does not merely call those who feel ready but equips those He calls, directly addressing their doubts and enhancing their inherent talents to fulfill His purposes.

The significance of these divine reassurances cannot be overstated. They underscore that God does not call the equipped but equips the called. The evolution of Moses from a humble shepherd riddled with self-doubt into a decisive leader was a gradual process. It unfolded through God's unwavering encouragement and support, a testament to divine patience and purposeful guidance. This story powerfully underscores the notion that our feelings of inadequacy do not render us incapable of fulfilling divine missions. On the contrary, it is precisely in these moments of perceived weakness that the strength of God is most potently manifested through us.

The struggle Moses faced with self-doubt is a profound reflection of the internal conflicts encountered in our own lives. The fear of feeling inadequate is a common challenge within our careers, relationships, and pursuing personal goals. Historical figures like Mahatma Gandhi and Eleanor Roosevelt, who overcame their battles with doubt and fear, serve as inspiring examples. Despite his initial shyness and insecurities, Gandhi became a pivotal leader in India's fight for independence. Similarly, Eleanor Roosevelt overcame significant self-doubt to become a powerful advocate for human rights. These examples highlight that feelings of inadequacy can be overcome through actionable steps: acknowledging your doubts without succumbing to them, seeking guidance and reassurance from prayer, mentorship, or a supportive community, reflecting on your past successes to boost your confidence, and taking calculated steps toward achieving your aspirations.

You may face daunting tasks or be outside your comfort zone in your personal journey. Reflect on these moments of self-doubt and consider how a divine calling might be at play. How have you responded to these challenges? The path to overcoming these feelings often involves seeking spiritual reassurance, guidance from mentors, or simply taking the first courageous step forward despite your fears. Remember, the story of Moses teaches us that God equips those He calls, providing us with the tools and support we need to fulfill our divine purposes.

PLAGUES OF EGYPT: DIVINE JUSTICE AND HUMAN HARDNESS

Imagine the profound shock of awakening to discover the Nile, your nation's lifeline, its waters as vital as the air you breathe, transformed into a river of blood. The fish, once teeming and vibrant, float lifelessly on the surface. The water, essential for drinking, irrigation, and daily rituals, has become a source of death, undrinkable, and emitting a stench that permeates every corner of Egypt. This catastrophic event began a series of ten plagues, each progressively more devastating than the last. These were not mere natural disasters; they were meticulously orchestrated signs of divine might aimed at demonstrating God's power over Egypt and its gods and bringing about justice for the enslaved Israelites. Yet, despite these awe-inspiring events, Pharaoh's heart remained unyielding. Despite the undeniable evidence of the miraculous unfolding before his eyes, he steadfastly refused to release the Israelites from bondage, as foretold in Exodus 7:3-4. This stubbornness transcends mere personal obstinance; it symbolizes a broader, more profound resistance—a quintessential example of human defiance against the manifest will of God. Even after such over-whelming signs, this hardening of Pharaoh's heart starkly illustrates the enduring struggle between divine commands and human rebellion.

The escalation of the plagues, from the initial turning of water into blood to the final, devastating death of the first-born, served a specific purpose. Each plague targeted a different aspect of Egyptian life and economy, gradually increasing in intensity. The initial plagues, such as frogs, gnats, and flies infestation, disrupted daily life. As Pharaoh continued to resist, the plagues became more destructive. Livestock died, boils afflicted humans and animals, and hail destroyed crops. Despite enduring these disasters, Pharaoh's resolve remained unshaken, precipitating the most grievous consequences: the firstborn's death (Exodus 7-12). This final plague was a profound manifestation of divine judgment, impacting every household in Egypt and ultimately breaking through Pharaoh's persistent refusal.

Grasping the full magnitude of the plagues requires a deep dive into ancient Egypt's cultural and religious fabric. Each plague wasn't just a calamity but a calculated challenge to the Egyptian gods, directly confronting and diminishing the powers they symbolized. The Nile's transformation into blood was not just a natural disaster but a pointed challenge to Hapi, the river deity considered Egypt's life-giver. Similarly, subsequent plagues targeted other key gods: Heqet, the fertility goddess with a frog's form, and Hathor, the bovine deity of nourishment, among others. These divine confrontations went beyond mere ecological disturbance; they were strategic assaults on the foundations of Egyptian belief and power, demonstrating the supremacy of Yahweh's authority. The ripple effects of these plagues shattered Egypt's spiritual confidence and societal structure, leading to economic turmoil and widespread suffering.

The impact on Egyptian society was profound. The plagues devastated the economy, agriculture, and public health. The death of livestock crippled food production, while the hail and locusts destroyed crops, leading to famine. The boils and darkness added to the misery, affecting the physical and psychological well-being of the people. The final plague, the death of the firstborn, struck at the heart of every family, leaving a trail of grief and despair. This series of events highlighted the futility of resisting divine will and the severe consequences of hard-heartedness.

The story of the plagues, drawing parallels to modern issues, offers valuable lessons on divine justice and human obstinacy.

We see various forms of resistance to justice and reform in today's world. Whether environmental degradation, social inequality, or political corruption, there are countless examples of individuals and systems resisting change. This obstinacy often leads to more tremendous suffering and injustice. The plagues remind us of the importance of humility and openness to divine guidance. Just as Pharaoh's resistance led to disaster, our stubbornness can hinder progress and exacerbate problems.

Reflect upon the contemporary struggles against injustice. Civil rights, environmental advocacy, and the pursuit of economic fairness have recurrently encountered formidable obstacles. Figures such as Martin Luther King Jr. and Nelson Mandela faced towering opposition in their quest for equity. Yet their unwavering resolve, fueled by a profound sense of divine calling and ethical conviction, propelled them forward. These instances mirror the biblical narrative's call to champion justice, even amidst formidable resistance.

Contemplate your stance when confronted with calls for justice. Do you resist transformative change, clinging to familiar patterns out of apprehension or obstinacy? Ponder the measures you might adopt to align more closely with divine will and the forces of change. This could entail a deeper exploration of social justice issues, actively listening to those directly impacted, and committing to actions that foster tangible improvements. The tale of the plagues invites a heartfelt introspection, urging us to confront our hesitations and to wholeheartedly commit to the path of justice and renewal, however challenging the journey may be.

THE RED SEA: MIRACLES IN IMPOSSIBLE SITUATIONS

Standing on the edge of the Red Sea, you can almost taste the salt in the air while a gentle breeze brushes against your face. Behind you, the dread sound of Pharaoh's approaching chariots grows louder—a relentless cacophony of metal and sand, accompanied by the desperate breathing of fast-approaching horses. Caught in this harrowing moment, the Israelites are overwhelmed by fear, turning to Moses in their terror. Their voices, heavy with the weight of despair, unite in a haunting refrain, "Was it because there were no graves in Egypt that you brought us to the desert to die?" (Exodus 14:11). This poignant question, born of deep anguish, resonates profoundly, echoing the Israelites' dire predicament. In this moment of utter desperation, Moses emerges as a bastion of unwavering faith. His steady, resolute voice cuts through the panic like a beacon of hope. "Do not be afraid. Stand firm and witness the salvation that the Lord will bring you today. The Egyptians whom you see today, you shall never see again. The Lord will fight for you; you have only to be silent and still" (Exodus 14:13-14). This profound declaration by Moses does not merely calm the rising storm of fear among the Israelites; it also ushers in the anticipation of a divine intervention, setting the stage for what is to unfold as one of the most monumental miracles documented in the Bible.

As Moses extended his hand toward the vast expanse of the Red Sea, a formidable east wind, as if summoned by the divine itself, began to sweep across the waters with unrelenting force. This was no ordinary meteorological phenomenon but a miraculous manipulation of nature, parting the seas to carve a path of salvation on dry ground. With each step the Israelites took on this newly forged passageway, flanked by imposing walls of water defying gravity on either side, their hearts swelled with an overwhelming sense of awe and reverence. This moment, vividly captured in Exodus 14:21-22, transcended a mere act of escape; it was a profound demonstration of God's boundless power and unwavering faithfulness when faced with what appeared to be an inescapable predicament. Through Moses, divine intervention carved a path to freedom. It highlighted a critical lesson: under God's guidance, no obstacle is too formidable, no barrier too great. The parting of the Red Sea is a testament to the belief that the seemingly impossible becomes possible with faith, illustrating that God's providential care can make a way where there seems to be none.

Exploring the historical and geographical context of the Red Sea crossing deepens our appreciation of its significance. The term "yam sup," present in the original Hebrew, is often translated as "Sea of Reeds," leading to diverse theories about its precise location, from the marshes above the Gulf of Suez to the Gulf of Aqaba. Yet, the core of this narrative is not its physical setting but the extraordinary act of divine intervention it portrays. Miracles within the faith tradition of the ancient Israelites were seen as direct interventions from God, transcending natural laws. These acts served not solely as profound demonstrations of God's power but as affirmations of His sovereign presence, reinforcing the belief in Yahweh as the supreme deity.

The Red Sea crossing is pivotal in the Exodus's broader narrative. It marks the definitive break from Egyptian bondage and the beginning of a journey towards the Promised Land. This event is repeatedly referenced throughout the Bible as a testament to God's ability to save and deliver. It was a cornerstone of Israelite identity, a reminder of their unique relationship with God and His capacity to intervene in human history. The miraculous crossing was a physical escape and a spiritual victory, symbolizing liberation from oppression and the dawn of a new covenant.

Reflecting on the Red Sea crossing, we can draw profound lessons about faith and reliance on divine intervention. We have all experienced "Red Sea" moments—situations that seem impossible to overcome. These moments test our faith and challenge us to trust in something greater than ourselves. Think about modern-day examples where faith is tested. Consider a person battling a severe illness, clinging to hope despite grim diagnoses. Or an individual facing insurmountable financial challenges, striving to believe in a breakthrough. These scenarios, though different, echo the desperation and subsequent deliverance experienced by the Israelites.

Trusting in God's timing and provision is crucial in these situations. The Israelites had to wait until the last possible moment for their deliverance, learning to trust that God's timing, though often incomprehensible, is perfect. This principle applies to our lives as well. When faced with daunting challenges, it's essential to cultivate a deep trust in divine timing and provision. This trust is not passive; it involves active faith, prayer, and a willingness to step forward even when the path is unclear.

Reflect upon the "Red Sea" moments in your lifetimes when obstacles appeared insurmountable. Yet, you witnessed remarkable turnarounds that could only be attributed to a higher power. Such instances serve as pillars of faith, reinforcing our trust in divine providence for the road ahead. Consider adopting regular spiritual practices like prayer and meditation to deepen your trust in this divine backing. Seek out and connect with faith communities for insight and encouragement, staying open to the remarkable ways divine assistance can reveal itself. The narrative of the Red Sea crossing beautifully illustrates that no predicament is beyond God's intervention; it teaches us that unwavering faith can indeed usher in wondrous deliverance.

MANNA FROM HEAVEN: TRUSTING GOD'S PROVISION

You are traversing an expansive desert, the relentless sun overhead, your body weary and hunger gnawing at your belly. This grueling scenario was not a fleeting hardship but an everyday existence for the Israelites as they navigated the wilderness for four decades. Within this severe landscape, a divine intervention manifested: manna, a peculiar, delicate substance that materialized with the dawn's dew. It was described as bearing the appearance of coriander seed, pale and round, and its taste reminiscent of honeyed wafers, serving as a palpable reminder of divine sustenance and fidelity. On each breaking day, the Israelites were tasked to gather precisely what they needed for that day alone, heeding the directives detailed in Exodus 16:4-5. This ritual of daily collection wasn't merely about physical nourishment; it was a sweeping spiritual exercise, continuously reminding them of the Lord's unwavering support and provision tailored to the rhythm of each new day.

The gathering of manna also underscored the significance of the Sabbath. The Israelites were instructed to collect a double portion on the sixth day, allowing them to rest on the seventh. As detailed in Exodus 16:23-26, this directive highlighted a miraculous aspect: the manna collected for the Sabbath did not spoil overnight, unlike the surplus on other days. This phenomenon underscored the sanctity of the Sabbath—a day dedicated to rest and divine worship. Observing the Sabbath was a testament to the Israelites' trust in God's provision and a reminder to rely on His timing and care.

Within the ancient Israelite context, manna was more than sustenance; it symbolized God's constant care and provision. In a culture where bread was a dietary staple, manna's daily appearance reinforced the concept of divine sustenance. This heavenly food nourished the Israelites physically and nurtured their faith, constantly reminding them of their reliance on God's grace. Through this daily act of trust and obedience in collecting manna, the Israelites learned the importance of depending on God for their daily needs, shaping their identity as a people of faith.

Reflecting on the significance of manna, we uncover profound insights into the essence of divine reliance for our everyday sustenance. In an era that champions autonomy and self-reliance, embracing the concept of daily dependence on divine grace presents challenges. Yet, just as the Israelites found their survival through the heavenly gift of manna, we are similarly invited to place our trust in divine provision for our needs. The narrative of George Müller, a devout Christian who founded and ran orphanages in England with no financial backing other than his unwavering faith and continuous prayer, exemplifies a contemporary parallel to this ancient lesson. Müller's experiences, marked by countless instances of timely divine intervention that met the needs of numerous children, serve as a testament to the enduring truth that reliance on divine provision remains as relevant and robust today as it was in the time of the Israelites.

Developing a mindset of gratitude and trust is a journey that involves intentional actions. Begin by recognizing the myriad ways divine provision touches your life each day. This recognition can be as straightforward as maintaining a gratitude journal, where you record both the monumental and the seemingly minor ways you experience God's presence and provision. Embrace contentment by shifting your focus to the abundance you possess rather than fixating on what remains beyond your grasp. This altered outlook fosters a deeper appreciation for the blessings you receive, allowing you to perceive God's hand in your life more clearly. Furthermore, dedicate time for rest and reflection, ideally observing a Sabbath. This practice pays homage to divine instruction and solidifies your reliance on God, a gentle reminder of the sacred promise to provide for you.

Contemplate the presence of divine provision in your life. Are you attuned to the 'manna' moments when God meets your needs in precisely the right measure and at the perfect time? Reflect on actions you might undertake to foster a spirit of gratitude and trust. This could include allocating moments daily to express thankfulness for God's generosity, seeking divine direction through prayer, and maintaining faith in the face of life's uncertainties. The narrative of manna from heaven eloquently illustrates the constancy and dependability of God's provision, encouraging us to place our trust in divine care for our daily sustenance.

In this chapter, we've explored how God miraculously provided for the Israelites, guiding them through moments of self-doubt, delivering justice through the plagues, parting the Red Sea, and providing manna in the wilderness. These stories remind us that God's provision and guidance are ever-present, even in the most challenging circumstances. As we transition to the next chapter, we'll continue to see how God's faithfulness unfolds in the lives of His people, offering lessons and insights that resonate with our own experiences today.

CHAPTER FOUR
WILDERNESS WANDERINGS

You are one in a community that has experienced the miraculous firsthand: the parting of the Red Sea creating a passage to freedom, the sky raining down manna for sustenance in your wilderness journey. Yet, even with these wonders, unease begins to permeate the group. Moses' prolonged absence on Mount Sinai seeds doubt among the people. During this period of uncertainty, as detailed in Exodus 32:1, the Israelites craved a tangible symbol of God's presence, compelling them to forge the golden calf.

In a moment of escalating impatience for a physical manifestation of the divine, the Israelites looked to Aaron, Moses' brother and high priest. At this crucial juncture, Aaron, succumbing to the people's demands, melted down their gold to form a calf. This mirrored the worship practices dedicated to the bull god Apis of Egypt and the Canaanite god Baal, symbols of power and fertility. This episode, detailed in Exodus 32:2-4, underscores Aaron's struggle to balance his leadership responsibilities with the populace's expectations. Moses' return to find his people engaged in idolatry provoked him to shatter the stone tablets bearing God's commandments, dramatically underscoring the gravity of their betrayal (Exodus 32:19-20).

In the ancient religious landscape of Israel, idolatry was not merely the worship of alternate deities; it constituted a profound breach of the covenant with Yahweh. Despite their solemn vow of undivided fidelity to God, the Israelites succumbed to the allure of a golden calf amidst their first encounter with uncertainty. This inclination towards idolatry was not isolated to Israel; it was a widespread phenomenon across the ancient Near East, where physical depictions of deities were commonplace, rendering the concept attractive and relatable. However, for the Israelites, crafting and venerating a golden calf represented an extreme form of spiritual infidelity—an outright renunciation of their faith and a regressive return to the spiritually hazardous traditions prevalent among their neighbors.

The creation and worship of the golden calf did more than breach the command against idolatry; it represented a fundamental misunderstanding of God's nature. By shaping God into a finite, visible object, the Israelites showed a profound lack of faith in His omnipresent, unseen presence. This act directly contravened the clear commandments laid out in Exodus 20:3-4, highlighting a misguided attempt to limit the limitless.

Today, while we might not bow down to golden statues, idolatry manifests more subtly and insidiously. Modern-day idols can be anything that takes God's rightful place in our hearts. Technology, for example, often distracts us from meaningful engagement with our faith and relationships. The constant lure of social media, the need to stay connected, and the quest for virtual validation can consume our attention and energy. Wealth and status are other prevalent idols. The relentless pursuit of financial success and societal recognition can quickly become the primary focus of our lives, overshadowing our spiritual growth and connection with God.

These distractions impact our spiritual growth and focus, much like the golden calf did for the Israelites. When our lives are filled with these modern idols, we find less time for reflection, prayer, and genuine connection with God. The story of the golden calf serves as a stark reminder of how easily we can be led astray by what is immediate and tangible, losing sight of what is eternal and divine.

Reflect on your own life. What "golden calves" or distractions are present? Is it the constant pull of your phone, the pursuit of career success, or perhaps the desire for social approval? These idols might not be as obvious as a golden statue, but they can be just as spiritually detrimental. Consider refocusing your priorities to align with your faith, perhaps by limiting your screen time or reassessing what truly matters.

Reflective Exercise

Take a moment to write down the distractions or "idols" that take up most of your time and energy. Reflect on why these are significant and how they might impact your spiritual growth. Then, jot down practical steps you can take to reduce their influence and refocus your priorities. This exercise can help you identify areas of your life that need realignment with your faith.

The story of the golden calf is a powerful lesson in the dangers of idolatry and distraction. It challenges us to examine our lives and consciously prioritize our relationship with God. We can cultivate a deeper, more focused spiritual life by recognizing and addressing our modern idols.

THE TWELVE SPIES: COURAGE AND FEAR IN DECISION-MAKING

You have been chosen for a mission critical to your people's future: scouting a land promised by God. This mission, filled with excitement and trepidation, was the reality for the twelve spies sent by Moses to explore Canaan, as detailed in Numbers 13:17-20. Their mission was all-encompassing—they were tasked with evaluating the land's fertility, gauging the strength of its inhabitants, and gathering evidence of the land's abundance.

Over forty days, they traversed this land of promise, meticulously examining everything from the soil's productivity to the local customs. This exploration was pivotal, serving not merely for tactical evaluation but also to reinforce the faith, bravery, and morale of the entire community of Israelites. Upon their return, the divergence in the reports of the twelve spies significantly impacted the Israelite community's morale and future decisions.

Caleb and Joshua, having witnessed the same scenes as their counterparts, chose to focus on the land's potential and promise. They reported back with optimism, underlining the land's fertility and the opportunities it presented. With conviction, Caleb expressed, "We should go up and take possession of the land, for we can certainly do it" (Numbers 13:30), his words echoing with confidence and faith in God's promise.

In stark contrast, the other ten spies presented a grim picture, overshadowed by fear and apprehension. Their observations, while factual, were tinted with a defeatist perspective. They spoke of the land's inhabitants as giants, insurmountable obstacles in their path. The cities, they reported, were fortified to the heavens, impregnable. "We can't attack those people; they are stronger than we are," they lamented (Numbers 13:31), painting a scenario of inevitable defeat.

This report, focusing solely on the challenges rather than the divine promise, sowed seeds of doubt among the Israelites. The community, swayed by the ten spies' fearful outlook, was plunged into despair. The fear was so overwhelming that it rekindled a desire to return to Egypt, a longing for the familiar bondage over the unknown promise (Numbers 14:1-4).

This pivotal moment underscored a crucial test of faith for the Israelites. Faced with the choice between embracing God's promise through faith and courage, as Caleb and Joshua advocated, or succumbing to fear and doubt, as the ten spies did, the community stood at a crossroads. This episode highlights the importance of perspective in facing challenges and serves as a profound lesson on the power of faith and the consequences of fear.

The mission of the twelve spies holds significant weight in the broader narrative of the Israelites' journey. Scouting the land of Canaan was a strategic move meant to prepare the Israelites for the challenges ahead. In ancient times, such reconnaissance missions were standard before military campaigns. The Israelites needed to understand the land's geography, resources, and potential threats. However, the cultural implications of fear and courage in ancient Israel were profound. Courage was not just a personal virtue but a communal necessity. The Israelites' identity was deeply tied to their faith in God's promises. The contrasting reports from the spies highlighted a pivotal moment where faith and fear collided.

Fear and courage have always played crucial roles in decision-making in ancient times and today. In our modern lives, we often face decisions that require us to choose between the comfort of the familiar and the uncertainty of the unknown. Consider the story of Malala Yousafzai, who faced immense personal risk to advocate for girls' education. Her courage in the face of danger not only changed her life but also inspired millions around the world. Similarly, the decision to start a new business, move to a new city, or stand up against injustice requires a leap of faith and the courage to face potential failure or opposition.

Faith and trust are essential in overcoming fear. Caleb and Joshua's confidence stemmed from their unwavering belief in God's promise. They saw the same giants and fortified cities as the other spies but chose to focus on God's power rather than the obstacles. This mindset is vital for us today. When faced with daunting decisions, reminding ourselves of past instances where faith led to positive outcomes can bolster our courage. Trusting in a higher purpose and seeking guidance through prayer and reflection can provide the strength to move forward despite fear.

Reflect on your own experiences with decision-making. When have you faced a decision that required courage? How did you respond? Consider the steps needed to cultivate courage and faith in your decision-making. This might involve identifying sources of fear, seeking support from trusted friends or mentors, and grounding yourself in your faith. Remember, like Caleb and Joshua, your perspective can shape your actions and the outcome. Choosing courage and faith over fear can lead to transformative and impactful decisions.

WATER FROM THE ROCK: FINDING HOPE IN DESPERATION

You are wandering through a barren desert, parched and desperate for water. Your children are crying, and the livestock are struggling to survive. This was the dire situation the Israelites faced in the wilderness. In Exodus 17:1-4, their desperation turned to complaints against Moses. "Why did you bring us up out of Egypt to make us and our children and livestock die of thirst?" they demanded. Seeing the weight of their despair, Moses cried out to God for help. His plea was not just a request for water but an urgent call for divine intervention to save desperate people.

God's response was both immediate and miraculous. He instructed Moses to take his staff and strike the rock at Horeb. "I will stand there before you by the rock at Horeb. Strike the rock, and water will come out of it for the people to drink," God promised (Exodus 17:5-6). Moses obeyed, and water gushed forth, providing life-sustaining relief for the entire community. This event was a powerful demonstration of God's faithfulness and provision in times of extreme need. It was a tangible reminder that even in the most desperate circumstances, God hears and responds to the cries of His people.

To fully appreciate this miraculous event, it's essential to understand the context and significance of where it occurred. The Sinai Peninsula, known for its harsh, dry terrain, made water exceedingly precious. Here, the search for water went beyond basic comfort—it was a matter of life and death. In this setting, water represents physical sustenance and carries deep symbolic meaning within their faith, signifying life, purification, and God's favor. Providing water from the rock is more than a simple provision; it's a powerful sign of God's unwavering loyalty to the Israelites during their wilderness journey. Each miracle, from manna to this miraculous water, acted as a foundation of their covenant with God, continually reminding them of His protective presence amidst their trials. The rock at Horeb becomes more than just a water source—it emerges as a symbol of God's ongoing guidance and the life-giving support He provides, even in the bleakest circumstances. Reflecting on this story, we can draw valuable lessons about finding Hope and trust in desperate situations. Life often brings us to our own "desert" moments—times of profound need, uncertainty, and despair.

These moments test our faith and challenge us to rely on something greater than ourselves. Consider modern-day examples where Hope and trust are crucial. Think of a family facing a medical crisis, unsure of the future but clinging to hope for healing. In this situation, relying on God's provision becomes a lifeline, a source of Hope transcending the immediate circumstances.

Embracing God's provision demands a transformative shift in how we view our circumstances. It necessitates recognizing that God is meticulously weaving the fabric of our journey beyond our sight and understanding. This kind of trust transcends mere passivity, engaging us in a dynamic relationship through prayer, active faith, and a relentless pursuit of divine direction.

Pause to reflect on the moments you've navigated your wilderness. Where did Hope find you? Was it in the embrace of your community, an encouraging word at just the right moment, or a revelation during prayer? Such encounters fortify our faith and serve as vivid reminders of God's unwavering loyalty and provision.

Reflect on methods to deepen your trust in God's provision during moments of desperation. Concentrating on God's previous acts of faithfulness can create a wellspring of Hope for navigating forthcoming trials. The narrative of water flowing from the rock represents a compelling affirmation of God's capacity to supply our needs through miracles, especially when circumstances seem dire. This story encourages us to place our trust in His provision and discover Hope in His steadfast support.

SERPENT ON THE POLE: HEALING AND FAITH

Imagine walking through a camp filled with the cries of your fellow Israelites, all suffering from deadly serpent bites. The scene is chaotic, filled with fear and despair. This was the harsh reality for the Israelites as they wandered through the wilderness. Their journey had been fraught with challenges, and their patience wore thin. In Numbers 21:4-6, their complaints reached a peak. "Why have you brought us up out of Egypt to die in the wilderness? There is no bread! There is no water! And we detest this miserable food!" Their grumbling triggered a severe consequence: God sent venomous snakes among them, and many Israelites died from the bites.

In response to the people's pleas for mercy, God instructed Moses to make a bronze serpent and set it on a pole. "Anyone who is bitten can look at it and live," God told Moses in Numbers 21:8-9. Looking up at the bronze serpent was more than a physical action; it was a profound act of faith and obedience. The bronze serpent became a symbol of healing, representing God's provision and mercy amid judgment. It wasn't the bronze serpent that healed them, but their faith in God's promise that looking at it would bring healing.

To grasp the profound meaning of the bronze serpent, it's crucial to consider its symbolism across various ancient Near Eastern cultures. Serpents, intriguingly, embodied dual notions of peril and cure. For example, the serpent signified royal power and divine protection in Egyptian lore, which is closely linked to the deity Wadjet. Similarly, Mesopotamian narratives portrayed serpents as entities that could safeguard or imperil humanity. This dichotomy wasn't lost on the Israelites; the bronze serpent ingeniously wove together these universal themes, transforming a familiar emblem of mortality into a divine conduit for salvation.

Within the tapestry of Israelite belief, this bronze figure stood as a testament to God's immediate and merciful response—a physical manifestation of divine will that transcended the typical associations of serpents with malice, redefining it as a source of life and deliverance. Symbols played a crucial role in ancient Israelite religion. They were tangible representations of divine truths and served as reminders of God's presence and power. The bronze serpent was one such symbol. It reminded the Israelites that healing and restoration came from looking to God in faith.

This event also foreshadowed the ultimate symbol of healing and salvation in Christian theology—the cross of Christ. In John 3:14-15, Jesus compared Himself to the bronze serpent, saying, "Just as Moses lifted the snake in the wilderness, so the Son of Man must be lifted up, that everyone who believes may have eternal life in him."

Reflecting on the story of the bronze serpent, we can draw valuable lessons about healing and faith. In modern times, we often face situations that require profound healing—whether it's physical illness, emotional trauma, or spiritual brokenness. Consider the story of someone battling cancer, enduring rounds of chemotherapy, and struggling to maintain Hope. Or think about someone grappling with the loss of a loved one, seeking emotional and spiritual healing. These situations, though different, share a common need for faith and trust in God's healing power.

Looking to God for healing and restoration involves more than just physical remedies. It requires a heart posture of faith and a willingness to trust in God's promises even when the outcome is uncertain. Just as the Israelites had to look up at the bronze serpent in faith, we are called to look to God in our times of need. This act of looking up is a powerful reminder that our healing comes not from the symbol itself but from the God who provides it.

Reflect on your own experiences with healing and faith. When have you experienced a need for healing in your life? How did you seek it? Perhaps you turned to prayer, sought support from your faith community, or found solace in scripture. Consider also how you can cultivate a deeper faith in God's healing power. This might involve daily practices of prayer and reflection, immersing yourself in God's promises, or seeking out testimonies of healing and restoration. The story of the bronze serpent invites us to trust in God's provision and to look to Him for our healing and restoration.

The Israelites' wilderness wanderings were marked by moments of profound challenge and divine intervention. From the idolatry of the golden calf to the fear and courage of the twelve spies to the desperate need for water and the healing provided by the bronze serpent, these stories offer timeless lessons for our own faith journeys. They remind us of the importance of faith, obedience, and trust in God's provision, even in the most challenging circumstances.

CHAPTER FIVE

JUDGES AND DELIVERANCE

Envision living in an era of turmoil and lawlessness, where a once harmonious community is fractured by internal conflicts and menaced by external threats. In this vortex of chaos, an unexpected figure of hope and steadiness arises, challenging the traditional image of leadership. Instead of a crowned sovereign or a seasoned warrior, this figure is a woman—Deborah. As a prophetess and judge, her existence and deeds craft a powerful tale of leadership, steadfast faith, and the remarkable impact of divine guidance.

DEBORAH'S LEADERSHIP: WOMEN IN FAITH

In an era characterized by male-dominated leadership, Deborah's rise as a figure of authority was revolutionary. She served as a prophetess, imbued with divine wisdom to guide Israel, and as a judge, entrusted with making pivotal decisions and offering sage advice. The distinctiveness of Deborah's role is underscored in the biblical narrative of Judges

4:6-9, where she calls upon Barak, a commander, to mobilize forces against the Canaanites' tyranny. Barak's insistence on Deborah's presence in the battle underscores her profound impact and the deep trust in her leadership capabilities. Deborah's role in military engagements was pivotal; she was actively involved, not merely a spectator. Her direct involvement in formulating strategies and overseeing their implementation was crucial. Her prophetic command to Barak, "Go! This is the day the Lord has given Sisera into your hands" (Judges 4:14), galvanized the Israelite forces. The resulting triumph over Sisera and his army was a testament to Deborah's leadership and the divine support that led them to victory. The battle was marked by a sudden heavy rain that confused the enemy and turned the tide in favor of Israel, leading to a decisive victory that ushered in forty years of peace.

Deborah's leadership is even more remarkable in its historical and cultural context. Female leadership was a rarity in ancient Near Eastern cultures. Societies were predominantly patriarchal, with men occupying most leadership roles. The concept of a female judge and military leader was almost unheard of. Judges in Israel were not just legal arbiters but also military leaders and spiritual guides. Deborah's dual role as a judge and prophet set her apart, making her a central figure in Israel's history. Her story is one of courage, wisdom, and divine inspiration, breaking the mold of traditional gender roles.

Drawing lessons from Deborah's story, we can see its relevance to modern discussions on female leadership and gender equality. Today, women continue to break barriers in various fields, from politics to business to religion. Consider figures like Malala Yousafzai, who advocates for girls' education despite facing immense opposition, or Jacinda Ardern, who leads with compassion and strength as the Prime Minister of New Zealand. These modern leaders, like Deborah, demonstrate that effective leadership transcends gender. They embody the principles of courage, wisdom, and justice, challenging societal norms and inspiring change.

In faith communities, recognizing and supporting female leadership is crucial. Women, like men, are endowed with unique gifts and callings that can enrich and strengthen the community. Deborah's story encourages us to value these contributions and create spaces where female leaders can thrive. This involves challenging traditional biases, providing opportunities for women to lead, and acknowledging the divine calling in their lives. It's about building a community where everyone's gifts are recognized and celebrated, regardless of gender.

Reflect on your views on leadership and gender equality. How do you view women's leadership roles within your faith community? Are there biases or preconceptions that need to be addressed? Consider the steps you can take to support and recognize female leaders. This might involve advocating for equal opportunities, mentoring young women, or simply being open to the diverse ways God calls individuals to lead. By embracing the lessons from Deborah's story, we can foster a more inclusive and empowering environment for all leaders.

Reflective Exercise

Take a moment to think about the women leaders in your community. Write down their names and the roles they serve. Reflect on how their leadership has impacted you and the community. Consider ways to support and encourage them, whether through words of affirmation, active involvement, or advocacy for greater recognition and opportunities. This exercise can help you appreciate the contributions of female leaders and inspire you to take concrete steps in supporting gender equality in leadership.

Deborah's story reminds us of the transformative impact of courageous and divinely inspired leadership. It invites us to reflect on our attitudes toward gender and leadership and take active steps toward creating a more inclusive and just community.

GIDEON'S FLEECE: SEEKING SIGNS AND DIVINE ASSURANCE

Picture yourself in Gideon's shoes, threshing wheat in a winepress to hide it from the Midianites. It was a time of oppression and despair for Israel. Suddenly, an angel of the Lord appeared, addressing him as a "mighty warrior" (Judges 6:12). Gideon was taken aback. How could he, from the weakest clan in Manasseh, be called to deliver Israel? This initial encounter set the stage for Gideon's requests for divine assurance. Feeling overwhelmed by the enormity of the task, Gideon sought signs from God to confirm his calling.

Gideon's first test with the fleece was straightforward. He placed a wool fleece on the threshing floor and prayed for a sign. "If there is dew only on the fleece and all the ground is dry, then I will know that you will save Israel by my hand" (Judges 6:37). The following day, the fleece was soaked with dew while the ground remained dry. This sign reassured Gideon, but his doubts lingered. So, he reversed the test: "Do not be angry with me. Let me make just one more request... this time make the fleece dry and let the ground be covered with dew" (Judges 6:39). God obliged, and the ground was wet with dew while the fleece remained dry. These signs were not just about physical phenomena; they were tangible confirmations of divine support, giving Gideon the courage to move forward.

Seeking signs and omens was a common practice in ancient Near Eastern cultures. People believed the divine realm interacted with the human world through natural phenomena, dreams, and other signs. In the Israelite religion, signs were seen as manifestations of God's will, providing guidance and assurance. Theological implications of seeking divine assurance are significant. It underscores the human need for reassurance and God's willingness to meet us in our doubts. Gideon's requests were not acts of faithlessness but expressions of his desire for confirmation. They reveal a dynamic relationship where God accommodates human insecurities, providing the necessary assurance to fulfill divine purposes.

In modern times, seeking signs from God remains a common practice among believers. People often seek divine guidance through various means, such as prayer, scripture, and circumstances. Consider the story of a person praying for a career change, seeking signs through job offers, conversations, or even dreams. While not as dramatic as Gideon's fleece, these signs serve a similar purpose. They provide reassurance and direction, helping individuals discern God's will. The challenge lies in discerning these signs and trusting in God's guidance. It's about balancing the desire for tangible assurance with faith in God's unseen hand.

Reflect on your own experiences with seeking signs and divine assurance. Have you ever prayed for a sign or confirmation from God? How did you discern it? These reflections can help you understand your relationship with divine guidance and how you seek assurance. Consider the steps needed to cultivate trust in God's guidance without relying solely on signs. Trusting in God's guidance often requires a leap of faith, believing He is at work even when signs are not immediately evident.

Reflective Exercise

Take a moment to think about a time when you sought a sign or confirmation from God. Write down the circumstances and how you felt during that period of waiting. Reflect on how you discerned the sign and what it meant for your faith journey. Consider how you can cultivate a deeper trust in God's guidance, even when signs are not as clear. This exercise can help you recognize the importance of faith and the role of divine assurance in your life.

Gideon's story is a potent example of seeking and receiving divine assurance. It reminds us that God meets us in our doubts, reassuring us to fulfill His purposes. Through his tests with the fleece, Gideon learned to trust in God's guidance, a lesson that continues to resonate with us today.

SAMSON'S STRENGTH: POWER AND WEAKNESS IN FAITH

Imagine a man of immense physical strength, capable of rending a lion with his bare hands, yet plagued by personal weaknesses and moral shortcomings. This figure is Samson, one of Israel's judges, who is celebrated for his unmatched might but also known for his vulnerabilities. His narrative intertwines acts of valor with moments of frailty, painting a nuanced picture of faith intertwined with human imperfection. The source of Samson's legendary strength was his Nazirite vow, detailed in Judges 13:5, wherein the angel of the Lord foretold that he would start liberating Israel from the Philistines. His unshorn hair was a symbol of his dedication to God. This commitment encompassed abstaining from wine, avoiding corpses, and never cutting his hair. These practices weren't merely ritualistic but emblematic of his extraordinary powers. Yet, despite his divine mission, Samson's journey was riddled with moral failings. One of the most glaring examples of Samson's weaknesses was his involvement with Delilah, a Philistine woman. Judges 16:4-6 recounts how Delilah, coaxed by the Philistine leaders with promises of silver, sought to discover the secret of Samson's strength. Her persistence eventually wore him down, leading him to reveal that his strength lay in his uncut hair. Delilah's betrayal, cutting his hair while he slept, resulted in Samson's capture and humiliation at the hands of the Philistines. This episode highlights the stark contrast between Samson's physical strength and susceptibility to temptation and manipulation. His downfall was not due to a lack of power but a failure to uphold his vow and recognize the vulnerabilities that came with his human desires.

The Nazirite vow, as detailed in Numbers 6:1-21, symbolized special dedication to God. Those who took this vow committed themselves to a higher standard of holiness, marked by specific restrictions. This vow was not a choice for Samson but a divine mandate given before his birth. His mother was instructed to follow the Nazirite restrictions during her pregnancy, and Samson was to be raised under the same vow. Judges in ancient Israel served as both deliverers and enforcers of God's will. They were expected to lead by example, embodying the principles of faith and righteousness. Samson's life, however, was a paradox. While he performed extraordinary acts of deliverance, his personal choices often contradicted the principles he was meant to uphold. The narrative of Samson illuminates the intricate dance between strength and vulnerability that leaders must navigate.

This theme resonates deeply in the stories of contemporary figures, such as Martin Luther King Jr., whose profound moral resilience in adversity was coupled with personal trials. The equilibrium between the demands of public leadership and the trials of private life is nuanced and fragile. Authentic leadership is anchored in strength, humility, and a willingness to be accountable. Acknowledging personal limitations and actively seeking accountability can avert the pitfalls that ensnared Samson. For those in leadership, it is imperative to stay rooted and comprehend that genuine power is found in recognizing and addressing personal vulnerabilities.

Reflect on the balance between your spiritual strengths and vulnerabilities. How do you ensure this equilibrium in your journey of faith? Recognize the areas where you feel strong, but also be aware of where you might be exposed to risks. Think about practical steps to promote accountability and humility in your leadership and influence. This could include seeking guidance from mentors, engaging in self-reflection, or implementing strategies to safeguard against your weaknesses. Samson's story is a powerful caution demonstrating that unchecked vulnerabilities can undermine even the most significant strengths.

Reflective Exercise

Take a moment to consider your leadership roles, whether in your community, workplace, or family. Write down your strengths and the areas where you feel most confident. Then, list your weaknesses and the potential risks they pose. Reflect on creating a balance, ensuring your vulnerabilities do not overshadow your strengths. Consider sharing this exercise with a trusted friend or mentor for additional insight and accountability.

Samson's story, filled with dramatic highs and lows, provides a rich tapestry of lessons on faith, power, and human frailty. It challenges us to reflect on our own lives and recognize that true strength comes from understanding and addressing our weaknesses while remaining faithful to our divine calling.

RUTH'S LOYALTY: DEVOTION AND REDEMPTION

Imagine the depth of sorrow and uncertainty Ruth must have felt as she faced the prospect of leaving her homeland. Widowhood had already upended her life, and now she stood at a crossroads with Naomi, her mother-in-law, who was also grieving the loss of her sons. Naomi urged Ruth to return to her people. Still, Ruth's response was a profound declaration of loyalty and devotion: "Where you go, I will go; where you stay, I will stay. Your people will be my people, and your God my God" (Ruth 1:16-17). This declaration wasn't just about staying with Naomi; it was a commitment to a new life, a new faith, and an uncertain future.

Ruth's commitment was not merely verbal but profoundly demonstrated through her actions. Upon arriving in Bethlehem with Naomi, she wasted no time seeking a means to support them both. She found herself gleaning in the fields of Boaz, a relative of Naomi's deceased husband, where her tireless work ethic and humility shone brightly. Struck by her loyalty to Naomi, Boaz took measures to ensure Ruth's protection and granted her privileges in the field beyond what was typically allowed (Ruth 2:2-3). For Ruth, laboring in the fields was not solely about sustenance; it was a profound demonstration of her love and commitment, a tangible manifestation of her deep loyalty.

The significance of Ruth's story is deeply rooted in the cultural and historical context of ancient Israel. In that society, widows were often vulnerable, lacking the protection and support of a husband. Family loyalty and kinship ties were paramount. Ruth, a Moabite, faced additional challenges as a foreigner. Her decision to stay with Naomi and integrate into Israelite society was a personal sacrifice and a bold step against cultural norms. The practice of levirate marriage, as outlined in Deuteronomy 25:5-10, plays a crucial role in Ruth's story. This custom required a close relative of a deceased man to marry his widow to preserve the family line. Recognizing his responsibility, Boaz agreed to marry Ruth, thus ensuring Naomi's family legacy would continue.

Ruth's story offers timeless lessons on loyalty, devotion, and redemption. In modern relationships, acts of loyalty and dedication often go unnoticed, yet they form the bedrock of enduring bonds. Consider the sacrifices made by a spouse who cares for their partner through a prolonged illness or the friend who stands by another through thick and thin. These acts of steadfast love reflect Ruth's example and remind us of the redemptive power of loyalty. Community and mutual support are equally important. Ruth's integration into Naomi's community and her support from Boaz highlight the importance of belonging and mutual aid. In moments of personal redemption, a community's support often makes all the difference.

Reflect on your own experiences with loyalty and devotion. When have you demonstrated unwavering loyalty in your relationships? Perhaps it was when you stood by a friend during a crisis or supported a family member in need. These moments, though they might seem small, carry profound significance. Consider how you can cultivate a spirit of devotion in your community. This might involve volunteering your time, offering support to those in need, or simply being present for the people you care about. Ruth's story encourages us to embrace the values of loyalty and devotion, recognizing their transformative power.

Reflective Exercise

Think about a relationship in which you have shown or received deep loyalty. Write down the actions demonstrating this loyalty and reflect on how they impacted you and the other person. Consider ways you can continue to nurture this spirit of devotion, whether through small acts of kindness, consistent support, or simply being there when it matters most. This exercise can help you appreciate the value of loyalty and inspire you to seek opportunities to demonstrate devotion in your relationships.

Ruth's unwavering loyalty and the resulting redemption she experienced offer a powerful narrative of commitment and love. Her story challenges us to reflect on our lives. It encourages us to embrace loyalty and devotion in our relationships and communities. By doing so, we can experience the redemptive power that comes from steadfast love and support.

As we move forward, let us remember Ruth's example, allowing her story to inspire us in our acts of devotion and loyalty.

CHAPTER SIX

KINGS AND PROPHETS

Picture a young boy nestled within the hallowed walls of a temple, his nights punctuated by a mysterious voice calling out to him in the silence. This wasn't a figment of his imagination but the lived experience of Samuel. Raised under Eli, the high priest's watchful eye, Samuel's early years were deeply entrenched in his faith's sacred rituals and texts. A life of devotion was not just a path laid out for him but a calling he embraced wholeheartedly. The Temple's sacred aura, with the lingering scent of incense and an air of solemn worship, shaped Samuel's youth, preparing him for his destiny as prophet and judge.

SAMUEL'S CALLING: LISTENING FOR GOD'S VOICE

While lying in the Temple, Samuel heard a voice calling his name one night. At first, he mistook it for Eli and ran to his mentor's side. "Here I am; you called me," he said. But Eli, confused, sent him back to bed. This happened three times until Eli realized God was calling the boy. He instructed

Samuel to respond, "Speak, Lord, for your servant is listening" (1 Samuel 3:4-10). When Samuel followed Eli's advice, God revealed a message to him, marking the beginning of Samuel's prophetic ministry. This initial encounter was not just a calling but an affirmation of Samuel's role as a significant figure in Israel's history.

Samuel's early heeding of God's summons showcases his exceptional character and eagerness to fulfill his divine purpose. Despite his youth, his readiness to heed and act upon God's call distinguished him from his peers. Samuel stood at the crossroads of two pivotal roles—prophet and judge—acting as a bridge between the divine and his people. As a prophet, he was the voice of God, tasked with delivering messages of guidance and correction to Israel—a stark contrast to the diminishing moral authority of the priestly class at the time. Samuel's dual capacity infused his leadership with spiritual insight and judicial wisdom, steering Israel through a transformative era.

Samuel's leadership marked a significant transformation, weaving spiritual insight and governance together and guiding the nation through its intricate moral and societal challenges. Prophets in ancient Israel held a crucial role, serving as intermediaries between God and the people. Their primary function was to convey God's messages, often addressing morality, social justice, and covenant faithfulness.

Unlike priests primarily concerned with rituals and temple services, prophets were called to speak out against corruption and lead the people back to God's ways. By Samuel's time, the priestly class had begun to lose its moral authority, paving the way for prophetic leadership to take center stage.

This significant shift emphasized the need for direct divine communication and accountability.

The decline of the priestly class and the rise of prophets like Samuel marked a pivotal moment in Israel's history. Priests, who were supposed to be the spiritual leaders, had become complacent and corrupt, as seen in the behavior of Eli's sons. In contrast, prophets like Samuel brought a renewed focus on righteousness and divine guidance. This transition highlights the dynamic nature of Israel's leadership and the importance of being attuned to God's voice. Prophets were not just religious figures; they were social reformers, calling the people to live according to God's covenant.

Listening to and recognizing God's voice remains a timeless challenge, a task made even more complex in the cacophony of our modern existence. Amidst the relentless din of our daily lives, discerning divine guidance emerges as a daunting endeavor. Yet, the narrative of Samuel illuminates a pathway through this spiritual labyrinth. Embracing regular spiritual disciplines such as prayer and meditation can act as a beacon, cutting through the noise to reveal moments of profound stillness. These practices invite tranquility into the chaos, aligning our hearts with the subtle yet profound whispers of the divine.

Similarly, the role of mentorship, exemplified in the dynamic between Samuel and Eli, emerges as vital. A spiritual mentor offers guidance, encouragement, and insight on the spiritual path. Contemplate your encounters with discerning and acting upon divine guidance to God's voice. When have you felt called by God? How did you recognize it? Perhaps it was a persistent thought, a sense of peace, or a confirmation through circumstances or trusted friends. Consider the steps to cultivate a more profound sensitivity to God's voice. This might involve setting aside regular quiet time or seeking guidance from a spiritual mentor. These practices can help you become more attuned to divine guidance and more responsive to God's call.

Reflective Exercise

Take a moment to reflect on a time when God called you. Write down the circumstances, your initial response, and how you eventually recognized it as a divine call. Consider what practices or changes you can implement to become more sensitive to God's voice. This exercise can help you identify patterns and cultivate a deeper awareness of God's presence and guidance.

SAUL'S DOWNFALL: PRIDE AND DISOBEDIENCE

Envision the gravity and excitement of being selected as the inaugural monarch of a new nation—a position replete with immense opportunity yet fraught with danger. The ceremonial anointing of Saul as Israel's first king was a landmark occurrence. Directed by divine mandate, Samuel consecrated Saul with oil, officially affirming him as the monarch (1 Samuel 10:1). This act transcended mere ceremonial tradition; it represented a divine sanction, unequivocally designating Saul as the chosen leader by God Himself. From the outset, Saul appeared destined for greatness. His tenure commenced with notable military triumphs, including a decisive victory against the Ammonites, which unified the Israelite people and solidified his leadership (1 Samuel 11:6-13).

However, Saul's early victories and growing confidence began to sow the seeds of his downfall. Success can be intoxicating, and Saul increasingly relied on his judgment rather than seeking divine guidance. Over time, his pride grew, distancing him from the humility that initially characterized his rule. One pivotal moment came when Saul, facing the Philistines, grew impatient, waiting for Samuel to offer sacrifices. Taking matters into his own hands, Saul performed the ritual himself, an act that was strictly the domain of the prophet (1 Samuel 13:8-14). This disobedience marked the beginning of God's rejection of Saul's kingship.

The final blow to Saul's reign came with his failure to fully obey God's command to annihilate the Amalekites and their possessions. God, through Samuel, had given explicit instructions to destroy everything, sparing nothing (1 Samuel 15:3). Yet, Saul spared King Agag and kept the best of the livestock, rationalizing his disobedience by claiming he intended to sacrifice the animals to God. When confronted by Samuel, Saul's disobedience and pride were laid bare. Samuel's words were stern and final: "To obey is better than sacrifice, and to heed is better than the fat of rams. For rebellion is like the sin of divination, and arrogance is like the evil of idolatry. Because you have rejected the word of the Lord, he has rejected you as king" (1 Samuel 15:22-23). This marked the irrevocable end of Saul's divine favor and the beginning of his tragic decline.

Grasping the full impact of Saul's fall requires understanding the pivotal role of kingship in ancient Israel. Before Saul, Israel was a loose federation of tribes, with judges stepping in as leaders in times of crisis. The shift to a monarchical system came from the people's desire for a unified leadership mirroring other nations. In this system, kings weren't merely political figures but were seen as divine agents charged with upholding God's covenant. Their duty was beyond governance; they were the spiritual linchpins of Israel, expected to guide the nation in adherence to sacred laws and maintain a vital connection with God. Saul's failure, therefore, was not merely a personal shortcoming but a breach of his covenantal duties. His pride and disobedience undermined the very foundation of his role. The shift from tribal confederation to monarchy was intended to provide stability and unity. However, Saul's actions highlighted the potential pitfalls of centralized power when not tempered by humility and obedience to God.

Reflecting on Saul's story, we see clear lessons on the dangers of pride and the importance of obedience in leadership. Modern history is replete with examples of leaders who fell from grace due to pride and disobedience. Consider Richard Nixon, whose involvement in the Watergate scandal led to his resignation. His fall resulted from pride and a belief that he was above the law. Similarly, CEOs and public figures engaging in unethical practices often ruin their careers and reputations. These modern parallels underscore the timeless truth that pride precedes a fall.

Humility and accountability are crucial in leadership. Saul's story reminds us that leaders must remain grounded and accountable, seeking guidance beyond their understanding. Reflect on your own experiences with pride. Have there been moments when pride clouded your judgment or led to decisions you later regretted? How did it impact your relationships or responsibilities? Consider the steps needed to cultivate humility and obedience in your leadership roles. This might involve seeking feedback, being open to correction, and prioritizing integrity over personal gain. By learning from Saul's downfall, we can strive to lead humbly, ensuring our actions align with our values and responsibilities.

DAVID AND GOLIATH: FACING LIFE'S GIANTS

Envision a youthful shepherd, accustomed to the solitary life of tending to his flock and warding off predators with nothing more than a simple sling and stones. Suddenly, he finds himself on a vast battlefield, confronting a towering warrior who stands over nine feet tall, armored from head to toe, and wielding a spear that seems more like a tree trunk than a weapon. This was the daunting reality for David as he stepped forward to face Goliath. Arrayed against the Israelite forces,

the Philistines had proposed a duel of champions to decide the conflict, a tactic not uncommon in the era's warfare, aiming to minimize the carnage of open battle.

The challenge from Goliath, the Philistine's fearsome giant, echoed menacingly across the Valley of Elah, daring any Israelite warrior to confront him. The Israelite ranks, including King Saul himself, were terrified at the prospect. Under these circumstances, David emerged with his unwavering belief in God. Presented with the opportunity to don King Saul's armor for the battle, David instead chose to face the giant with his sling and stones—a decision born from his faith in God's protection. He famously declared, "The Lord who delivered me from the paw of the lion and the paw of the bear will deliver me from the hand of this Philistine" (1 Samuel 17:37), affirming his trust in divine intervention over earthly armor.

David's trust in God over physical armor is a powerful testament to his faith. He understood that his true strength came not from weapons or armor but from his relationship with God. As he approached Goliath, David's words were filled with conviction: "You come against me with sword and spear and javelin, but I come against you in the name of the Lord Almighty" (1 Samuel 17:45). This declaration wasn't just bravado; it was a profound expression of faith. David knew that the battle belonged to God. He took a stone from his bag, slung it, and struck Goliath on the forehead. The giant fell face down, and David used Goliath's sword to complete the victory (1 Samuel 17:50).

David's triumph over Goliath transcends mere battlefield victory; it heralded his ascent to future kingship, embodying his remarkable bravery and unwavering faith. The menace posed by the Philistines was an enduring challenge for Israel, making the Valley of Elah not just a battleground but a crucible of destiny. In overcoming Goliath, David achieved more than a tactical win; he ignited a spark of hope and unity among the Israelite ranks. This act of valor against seemingly insurmountable odds did not merely define a moment; it marked a pivotal shift in Israel's narrative. The practice of deciding battles through single combat was prevalent in the ancient Near Eastern military strategy, serving as a means to avert widespread slaughter, with the outcome often setting the course for broader conflicts. In this light, David's conquest was a personal milestone and a moment of profound national significance, transforming the tide of Israel's history.

Drawing lessons from David's experience, we see the importance of courage, faith, and overcoming obstacles. In our modern lives, we face our own "giants"—insurmountable challenges. These giants can paralyze us with fear, whether it's a health crisis, financial difficulties, or personal struggles. David's story teaches us that courage and faith can make all the difference. It's about facing challenges head-on and trusting in a power greater than ourselves. In the contemporary world, stories of courage and faith continue to inspire.

Malala Yousafzai, whose unwavering stand for educational rights in the face of Taliban threats, won her the Nobel Peace Prize and spotlighted the power of steadfast belief in one's principles. Similarly, despite being born without limbs, Nick Vujicic has touched countless individuals worldwide through his motivational speeches and writings, demonstrating that physical limitations are no match for the human spirit buoyed by faith. These modern narratives echo David's ancient victory, illustrating that the seemingly insurmountable obstacles in our paths can be overcome with courage and faith.

Reflect on the giants you are currently facing in your life. What challenges seem insurmountable? How do you respond to them? Are there ways you can cultivate a deeper trust in God to help you overcome these challenges? Consider setting aside time for prayer and reflection, seeking support from your faith community, or immersing yourself in scripture that reinforces God's promises. David's story is a powerful reminder that no challenge is too great when we trust God and face our giants with courage and faith.

SOLOMON'S WISDOM: DIVINE WISDOM AND HUMAN FOLLY

Imagine being young and suddenly thrust into the role of a ruler over a vast nation. This was Solomon's reality when he became King of Israel. One night, God appeared to Solomon in a dream and said, "Ask for whatever you want me to give you" (1 Kings 3:5). Instead of asking for wealth, long life, or the defeat of his enemies, Solomon asked for wisdom. He desired "a discerning heart to govern your people and to distinguish between right and wrong" (1 Kings 3:9). Pleased with Solomon's request, God granted him unparalleled wisdom, riches, and honor. This divine gift began Solomon's reign and reputation as the wisest man on Earth.

Under Solomon's leadership, Israel experienced unprecedented prosperity and stability. One of his most significant accomplishments was the construction of the Temple in Jerusalem. This project took seven years to complete (1 Kings 6:1-38). This magnificent structure became the center of Israelite worship and a symbol of God's presence among His people. The Temple's grandeur, detailed craftsmanship, and precious materials showcased the nation's wealth and Solomon's dedication to honoring God. Extensive building projects, trade expansions, and the establishment of solid alliances through marriages with foreign princesses also marked Solomon's reign.

However, Solomon's alliances, particularly foreign marriages, eventually led to his downfall. Despite his wisdom, Solomon's heart turned away from God as he grew older. Influenced by his foreign wives, he began to worship other gods and built high places for these deities (1 Kings 11:1-11). This idolatry angered God, who had explicitly warned Solomon against such practices. The very wisdom that had brought Solomon success became overshadowed by his folly. His divided heart led to the eventual division of the kingdom after his death, illustrating the dangers of compromising one's faith for political gain.

Solomon's reign stands out in Israel's history for its economic and political stability. Under his rule, Israel became a powerful and prosperous nation with thriving trade networks and a robust military presence. The wealth accumulated during Solomon's reign allowed grand architectural projects and cultural advancements. However, the cultural and religious influences of Solomon's foreign marriages introduced syncretism, blending Israelite worship with pagan practices. This blending diluted the purity of Israel's faith and set a precedent for future kings struggling with similar temptations.

Reflecting on Solomon's story, we see the delicate balance between divine wisdom and human folly. Solomon's request for knowledge and subsequent achievements highlight the importance of seeking God's guidance in leadership. However, his eventual turn to idolatry underscores the dangers of losing sight of one's spiritual integrity amidst success. Modern leaders, too, face the challenge of balancing wisdom with humility. Consider the example of Steve Jobs, whose visionary leadership transformed the tech industry but whose personal flaws and management style also drew criticism. Or think of political figures who, despite initial success, succumb to corruption and ethical lapses. These stories remind us that wisdom must be coupled with spiritual integrity to avoid the pitfalls of folly.

Reflect on moments in your life when you have experienced divine wisdom. Perhaps it was a decision that brought unexpected clarity or a situation where you felt guided beyond your understanding. How did you recognize it as divine wisdom? Consider also how you can guard against the pitfalls of folly in your personal and professional life. This might involve regular self-reflection, seeking accountability from trusted friends or mentors, and staying grounded in your faith. Solomon's story is a powerful reminder that wisdom, while invaluable, must be nurtured and guarded to maintain spiritual integrity.

Reflective Exercise

Take a moment to reflect on a time when you experienced divine wisdom. Write down the circumstances, your initial thoughts, and the outcome. Consider what practices or changes you can implement to guard against folly and maintain spiritual integrity. This exercise can help you identify patterns and deepen your awareness of God's wisdom and guidance.

Solomon's life, filled with divine wisdom and human folly, offers a profound lesson on maintaining spiritual integrity amidst success. As we move forward, we'll continue exploring the lives of Israel's kings and prophets, each offering unique lessons and insights.

CHAPTER SEVEN
EXILE AND RETURN

You find yourself atop a mountain, encircled by multitudes who have forsaken their ancestral faith in favor of Baal, a deity alien to their heritage. In this scenario, you're the solitary figure beckoning them toward reclamation of their devotion to the true God. Such was the circumstance confronting Elijah, a prophet amidst the tumult of Israel's saga. The Northern Kingdom found itself trapped in the clutches of idol worship, a situation primarily attributed to King Ahab and Queen Jezebel's fervent endorsement of Baal. Amidst this widespread renunciation of faith, Elijah's steadfast faith and courage in confronting widespread disbelief serve as a powerful example of the strength of unwavering faith amidst significant opposition.

ELIJAH'S CHALLENGE: STANDING FIRM IN FAITH

Elijah's confrontation with the prophets of Baal on Mount Carmel is one of scripture's most dramatic and powerful episodes. As described in 1 Kings 18:20-24, Elijah called for a showdown to prove who the true God was. He challenged King Ahab to gather all of Israel and the 450 prophets of Baal on Mount Carmel. The proposition was simple: both Elijah and the prophets of Baal would prepare a sacrifice, but neither would light the fire. The true God would be the one who answered by sending fire to consume the offering. This challenge directly affronted Baal, considered the God of storms and lightning. If Baal were real, he should be able to send fire from the sky.

The preparation of the altars was a significant part of this confrontation. Elijah allowed the prophets of Baal to go first. They prepared their bull and began calling on Baal from morning till noon, shouting and dancing around the altar. But there was no response. Elijah, with a mix of sarcasm and confidence, mocked them, suggesting that perhaps Baal was deep in thought, busy, traveling, or maybe even sleeping and needed to be awakened (1 Kings 18:27). The prophets of Baal intensified their efforts, slashing themselves with swords and spears until their blood flowed. Still, there was no answer (1 Kings 18:28-29). The contrast between the frenzied, desperate actions of the prophets of Baal and Elijah's calm, assured demeanor could not have been starker.

When it was Elijah's turn, he rebuilt the altar of the Lord with twelve stones, representing the twelve tribes of Israel. He dug a trench around it, arranged the wood, cut the bull into pieces, and laid it on the wood. To ensure there was no doubt about the authenticity of the miracle to come, Elijah had the people pour four large jars of water over the offering and the wood three times until the water filled the trench (1 Kings 18:33-35). Then, at the time of sacrifice, Elijah stepped forward and prayed, "Lord, the God of Abraham, Isaac, and

Israel, let it be known today that you are God in Israel and that I am your servant and have done all these things at your command. Answer me, Lord, answer me, so these people will know that you, Lord, are God, and that you are turning their hearts back again" (1 Kings 18:36-37).

God's response was immediate and miraculous. Fire from the Lord fell from heaven and consumed the burnt offering, the wood, the stones, the soil, and even the water in the trench (1 Kings 18:38). The people fell prostrate and cried, "The Lord—he is God! The Lord—he is God!" (1 Kings 18:39). This miraculous demonstration of God's power was a turning point, momentarily bringing the people back to the true God and leading to the execution of the false prophets of Baal.

The significance of Elijah's challenge cannot be overstated. In ancient Israelite religion, the worship of Baal had become widespread in the Northern Kingdom due to political and cultural influences, mainly through Ahab's marriage to Jezebel, a devoted worshiper of Baal. Baal worship included rituals that were deeply ingrained in the surrounding cultures, making it a significant threat to the monotheistic worship of Yahweh. Prophets like Elijah were called to confront these idolatrous practices and call the people back to their covenant with the true God. Elijah's boldness in challenging Baal's prophets and his unwavering faith in God's power highlighted the role of prophets as defenders of the faith and instruments of divine intervention.

Reflect on your own experiences with standing firm in faith. When have you faced opposition to your faith? How did you respond? Consider the steps to strengthen your resolve to stand firm in your beliefs. Remember, like Elijah, you are not alone. Your faith is supported by a community and a history of those who have stood firm before you.

Reflective Exercise

Pause and recall an instance where others challenged your faith. How did you navigate that opposition, and what insights did you gain from that ordeal? Contemplate the steps needed to fortify your faith and determination, like seeking guidance from those who embody the virtues you admire. This reflective exercise is designed to aid in constructing a solid foundation that supports you in steadfastly maintaining your beliefs when faced with adversity. Elisha's Miracles: Faith in Action

ELISHA'S MIRACLES: FAITH IN ACTION

There was a time when miracles were not just stories but tangible events that demonstrated God's power and presence. Elisha, a prophet who succeeded Elijah, performed numerous miracles that affirmed God's authority and provided for the needs of the people. One of his first miracles was the purification of poisoned water at Jericho. The city's people came to Elisha, explaining that while their town was well-situated, the water was bad, causing death and unfruitfulness (2 Kings 2:19-22). Elisha asked for a new bowl filled with salt and threw it into the spring. He declared, "This is what the Lord says: 'I have healed this water. Never again will it cause death or make the land unproductive.'" Instantly, the water was purified, demonstrating God's ability to turn a dire situation into one of life and abundance.

Another significant miracle Elisha performed was the multiplication of the widow's oil. In 2 Kings 4:1-7, a widow of a prophet came to Elisha, desperate because a creditor was coming to enslave her two sons to pay off her debt. Elisha asked her what she had in her house, and she replied that she had only a small jar of olive oil. Elisha instructed her to gather as many empty jars as she could from her neighbors, then go inside her house and pour oil into all the jars. She did as she was told, and the oil miraculously kept flowing until every jar was filled. Elisha then told her to sell the oil, pay her debts, and live on what was left. This miracle saved her sons from slavery and provided for their future, illustrating God's provision in times of need.

Among the myriad of wonders Elisha is credited with, the revival of the Shunammite woman's son stands out as particularly moving. The narrative unfolds in 2 Kings 4:32-37, where Elisha has nurtured a bond with a well-to-do Shunammite woman, who generously offered him lodging during his travels. As a token of his appreciation, Elisha foretold the birth of a son to her—a prediction that materialized but was tragically short-lived when the boy unexpectedly passed away. Distraught, the woman placed her son's body on the bed reserved for the prophet and sought Elisha's help. Upon his arrival, Elisha turned to prayer, then laid upon the child, who, after sneezing seven times, miraculously returned to life. This event underscores God's dominion over life and mortality and illustrates Elisha's instrumental role in manifesting God's miraculous deeds.

In the society of ancient Israel, miracles were not mere spectacles; they served a critical function in affirming the authority of prophets. The extraordinary deeds of Elisha went beyond showcasing divine power—they were intricately woven into the very fabric of daily life, addressing the essential needs for sustenance, health, and safety. These acts of wonder demonstrated God's deep investment in the welfare of His followers. Furthermore, they played a pivotal role in upholding the tradition of prophecy, solidifying Elisha's position as Elijah's rightful heir, and ensuring the unbroken flow of divine wisdom and guidance. The social and economic implications of Elisha's miracles were profound. The purification of the water at Jericho turned a life-threatening situation into prosperity. The multiplication of the widow's oil provided financial stability and security for a vulnerable family. The Shunammite woman's son's resurrection restored hope and affirmed life's sanctity. These miracles were acts of divine intervention that met people where they were, addressing their immediate needs and reinforcing their faith in God's provision.

Reflecting on Elisha's miracles, we see the importance of active faith and divine intervention in our lives. Modern challenges often require us to live out our faith in tangible ways, trusting God's power to intervene in our circumstances. Consider the story of someone who experiences miraculous healing after fervent prayer or the community that comes together to support a family in need, witnessing what they perceive as divine provision. These modern acts of faith and divine intervention echo the miracles performed by Elisha, reminding us of God's ongoing involvement in our lives.

Reflect on your own experiences with active faith and divine intervention. When have you witnessed or experienced a "miracle" in your life? Perhaps it was a moment when everything seemed lost, and a solution appeared out of nowhere, or when you felt a profound sense of peace and guidance amidst chaos. Consider how you can put your faith into action in your daily life. This might involve small acts of kindness, stepping out in faith to help someone in need, or simply trusting God with the uncertainties you face. Remember, like Elisha, your faith can be a powerful catalyst for witnessing God's miracles in your life and the lives of others.

Reflective Exercise

Take a moment to write down a time when you witnessed or experienced a miracle. How did it impact your faith? Reflect on ways you can actively live out your faith daily, whether through acts of service, prayer, or trusting God with your challenges. This exercise can help you recognize the importance of active faith and encourage you to remain open to divine intervention.

DANIEL IN THE LION'S DEN: FAITH UNDER PERSECUTION

You find yourself in a foreign land, far removed from the comforts of home and the community that shares your beliefs. In this unfamiliar and often hostile environment, your faith is not just misunderstood—it's directly challenged by those in power. This was the reality for Daniel, a Jewish exile in Babylon, whose story is a testament to steadfast faith in the face of adversity. His most famous challenge occurred when King Darius, influenced by the cunning plans of Daniel's rivals, established a decree that forbade prayer to any deity or man other than the king for thirty days (Daniel

6:6-10). This decree was a deliberate trap to exploit Daniel's commitment to his daily prayers. Yet, Daniel remained undeterred. Despite the imminent threat, he continued his practice of praying openly to God, showcasing a profound faith that stood tall against the forces of oppression.

Daniel's act of defiance swiftly caught the attention of his adversaries, who wasted no time bringing his breach of the decree to the king's notice, culminating in Daniel's apprehension. King Darius, who held Daniel in high esteem, was in a quandary. Despite his regard for Daniel, he was ensnared by the immutable decree of the Medes and Persians. With a heavy heart, he ordered Daniel to be cast into the lion's den (Daniel 6:11-16) while harboring a glimmer of hope that Daniel's God would intervene.

This critical juncture underscored the clash between the king's admiration for Daniel and the imperatives of his royal duty. Furthermore, it prepared the ground for what was to become an awe-inspiring display of divine safeguarding. The following day, King Darius hurried to the lion's den, calling out to Daniel. To his relief, Daniel was unharmed. Daniel explained that God had sent an angel to shut the lions' mouths because he was found blameless before God and had committed no crime against the king (Daniel 6:19-23). This miraculous deliverance was a powerful testament to God's protection and Daniel's faith. The king then ordered Daniel's accusers and their families to be thrown into the lion's den, where they met a gruesome fate. This story ends with King Darius issuing a decree that all in his kingdom must fear and reverence the God of Daniel, acknowledging His power and sovereignty.

Understanding the historical and cultural context of Daniel's story enriches our appreciation of his faith. The Babylonian exile was a period of immense challenge for the Jewish community. They were uprooted from their homeland and faced the challenge of maintaining their religious identity in a foreign culture. Babylon's political and spiritual climate was complex, marked by a pantheon of gods and the king's absolute authority. Jewish officials like Daniel held significant positions in the Babylonian administration, often navigating a delicate balance between their faith and duties. Daniel's story highlights the tension between staying true to one's beliefs and adapting to a foreign culture.

Daniel's experience resonates with the modern challenges of maintaining faith and integrity in hostile environments. Consider the example of Dietrich Bonhoeffer, a German pastor who opposed the Nazi regime and was executed for his resistance. Like Daniel, Bonhoeffer maintained his faith and integrity despite severe persecution. Another example is that of modern-day Christians in regions where religious persecution is rampant. Their stories of enduring faith amidst danger remind us of the importance of standing firm in our beliefs, even when faced with opposition.

Reflect on your own experiences with persecution and maintaining faith. When have you faced challenges to your faith in a hostile environment? How did you respond? Consider the steps needed to keep your integrity and trust in God amidst persecution. Like Daniel, your faith and integrity can be a powerful witness to others, even in the most challenging circumstances.

Reflective Exercise

Take a moment to write about a time when you faced challenges to your faith. How did you handle the situation, and what did you learn from it? Reflect on ways to strengthen your faith and maintain your integrity in hostile environments. This exercise can help you prepare for future challenges and reinforce your commitment to keeping your faith amidst adversity.

JONAH'S RELUCTANCE: OBEDIENCE AND DIVINE MERCY

Consider the profound discomfort of delivering a divine message to those you loathe. Such was the predicament faced by Jonah as God directed him to journey to Nineveh, the heartland of Assyria and a notorious adversary of Israel. Rebelling against this command, Jonah sought refuge in flight, setting sail for Tarshish to elude God's directive and His presence. The narrative in Jonah 1:3-4 portrays this act as a physical retreat and a spiritual evasion from a challenging divine assignment. Amidst his escape, God unleashed a fierce tempest that threatened to dismantle the vessel. In their panic, the crew resorted to casting lots, a practice that inevitably singled out Jonah as the cause of their turmoil. Confronted with the severity of his defiance, Jonah proposed that he be sacrificed and cast into the tumultuous sea, believing his action would quell the storm's rage.

Swallowed by a great fish, Jonah spent three days and three nights in its belly. During this time, he prayed a heartfelt prayer of repentance, acknowledging God's sovereignty and expressing his desperation (Jonah 2:1-10). His prayer is a moving expression of remorse and a plea for deliverance. God, in His mercy, commanded the fish to vomit Jonah onto dry land. This miraculous deliverance was not just about Jonah's physical survival but also a profound lesson in divine mercy and the possibility of redemption even after disobedience.

Jonah obeyed God's command and went to Nineveh, proclaiming that the city would be overturned in forty days unless they repented (Jonah 3:4-10). To Jonah's astonishment, the people of Nineveh believed in God. From the greatest to the least, they declared a fast and put on sackcloth as a sign of their repentance. Even the king of Nineveh arose from his throne, covered himself with sackcloth, and issued a decree for everyone to call urgently on God. Their genuine repentance moved God to relent and withhold the destruction He had planned. This turn of events highlights God's boundless mercy and willingness to forgive even those we might consider undeserving.

Grasping the full significance of Jonah's task necessitates an exploration of the historical and cultural backdrop. Nineveh, the Assyrian empire's capital, was a formidable force in the ancient world, celebrated for its military might and feared for its aggressive campaigns of conquest. The Assyrians' reputation for harshness and their imperial ambitions placed them at odds with Israel, fostering a deep-seated animosity. This backdrop made Jonah's assignment to Nineveh challenging and profoundly distasteful. As a nexus of power and a hub of pagan worship, Nineveh epitomized the antithesis of Israelite values and beliefs. Jonah's hesitation was rooted in more than apprehension; it was fueled by a profound aversion to the Assyrians, whom he deemed unworthy of divine compassion.

Jonah's narrative offers deep insights into the essence of obedience and the expansiveness of divine mercy. In contemporary contexts, we are often confronted with the necessity to heed challenging directives, be it advocating for justice amid adversity, undertaking substantial personal transitions, or offering forgiveness to those who have inflicted harm.

Consider the story of Corrie ten Boom, a Holocaust survivor who displayed profound obedience to God's call for forgiveness by pardoning a former Nazi guard. This act, which caused her deep emotional pain, powerfully showcases the strenuous obedience sometimes required of us by God. Facing the challenge of extending mercy in our relationships demands that we rise above our resentments, opening our hearts to the potential for transformation and renewal.

Reflect on your own experiences with obedience and mercy. When have you struggled with obeying a complex command from God? Perhaps it was a call to forgive, to serve in an uncomfortable setting, or to make a life-altering decision. How did you respond, and what did you learn from the experience? Consider also how you can recognize and extend God's mercy in your interactions with others. This might involve letting go of past hurts, offering a second chance, or simply choosing to see the good in someone. Jonah's story challenges us to embrace obedience even when it's hard and to extend mercy even when it's undeserved.

Reflective Exercise

Take a moment to write down a time when you struggled with obeying a complex command from God. Reflect on how you handled it and what you learned. Determine practical steps to recognize and extend God's mercy in your relationships. This exercise can help you internalize the lessons from Jonah's story and apply them to your own life.

Jonah's experience underscores the importance of obedience and the vastness of divine mercy. His story reminds us that God's plans often extend beyond our understanding and that His mercy knows no bounds. As we reflect on Jonah's journey and our own, let's strive to obey God's commands and extend mercy to those around us, recognizing that we are all recipients of His grace.

CHAPTER EIGHT

WISDOM LITERATURE

Consider the profound sense of loss that would come from having everything you value, your fortune, your family, and your health stripped away in one catastrophic moment. This is Job's ordeal, a testimony to enduring faith amid extreme adversity. Initially, Job's life was full of abundant wealth and devout faithfulness. He is immensely prosperous, with extensive herds and a large, close-knit family. His devotion to God is evident in his regular sacrifices for his children's spiritual protection. Yet, this idyllic existence is shattered by a series of tragic events. Within a single day, Job's world is turned upside down as he faces the loss of his property to thieves, the murder of his servants, and the death of his children due to a natural disaster (Job 1:1-3, 13-19). These devastating losses serve as a backdrop for an intense exploration of the nature of suffering and the essence of faith.

Job's initial response to his suffering was profound lament and questioning. In Job 3:1-26, he curses the day of his birth, expressing a deep sense of despair. His words are raw and honest, revealing the depth of his anguish. Job's expression of sorrow transcends mere outcry; it embodies a quest for clarity amidst turmoil. He grapples with his suffering, seeking understanding for his misfortunes despite his blameless existence. This intense emotional release is a testament to the simultaneous existence of faith and suffering. Job's readiness to articulate his anguish and bewilderment illustrates that questioning the divine does not denote frailty in belief but rather signifies an authentic engagement with God.

The dialogues between Job and his friends, spanning chapters 4 to 27, form the heart of the Book of Job. These conversations offer various perspectives on suffering and divine justice. Job's friends—Eliphaz, Bildad, and Zophar—insist that his suffering must result from some hidden sin, adhering to the retribution theology prevalent in their culture. They argue that God is just and, therefore, Job's misfortunes must be a form of punishment. Job, however, maintains his innocence and challenges their simplistic explanations. He insists that his suffering is not a result of personal sin but a mystery that defies easy answers. These dialogues highlight the limitations of human understanding and the complexity of divine justice.

The Book of Job holds a special place in ancient Near Eastern literature. It is often compared to other wisdom texts, such as the Babylonian poem known as the "Babylonian Job." Like Job, this poem explores a righteous man's suffering and the gods' seeming capriciousness. However, while the Babylonian text grapples with the unpredictability of fate, the Book of

Job delves deeper into the nature of divine justice and the mystery of God's ways. The role of the "Satan" figure in Job is also significant. In the prologue, Satan appears as a member of the divine council, challenging Job's piety by suggesting that it is rooted in his prosperity. This portrayal of Satan evolves in later Jewish teachings., becoming more closely associated with the adversary figure we recognize today.

Job's story critiques the simplistic belief that suffering is merely the consequence of one's sins. It shifts the focus towards acknowledging God's unfathomable sovereignty and the enigmatic nature of His decisions. The story meticulously illustrates that hardships aren't always punishments but can also serve as a canvas for the manifestation of divine purposes, aligning with the teachings of Jesus in John 9:2-3. Through the engaging dialogues and the divine discourse that concludes the tale, the text invites readers to recognize the bounds of human insight and the wisdom in placing trust within God's overarching design. Job's final act of conceding his inability to fully grasp divine logic and repentance for daring to challenge it underscores a lesson in humility and unwavering faith amidst life's trials.

Modern examples of individuals who have demonstrated faith amidst suffering can provide us with inspiration and perspective. Consider the story of Joni Eareckson Tada, who became a quadriplegic after a diving accident. Despite her physical limitations and the emotional struggles that followed, Joni has remained steadfast in her faith, becoming an influential author and advocate for people with disabilities. Like Job's, her story reminds us of the importance of maintaining integrity and trust in God during difficult times.

It demonstrates that faith can provide strength and hope, even in the darkest moments.

Reflect on your own experiences with suffering and faith. When have you faced significant trials in your life? How did you respond? Consider the steps needed to maintain faith and trust in God amidst suffering. This might involve finding inspiration in the stories of others who have endured similar challenges. Remember, Job's story teaches us that suffering is not always a punishment but can be a profound opportunity to deepen our faith and understand God's mysterious ways.

PSALMS OF DAVID: EMOTIONAL HONESTY IN PRAYER

Picture for a moment sitting alone in the quiet of the night, your heart heavy with sorrow, feeling as if the world has turned its back on you. This is the emotional landscape of many of David's psalms. David's psalms cover many emotions, from despair and lament to joy and thanksgiving. Take Psalm 22:1-2, for instance, where David cries out, "My God, my God, why have you forsaken me?" These words echo the depths of human despair, expressing a feeling of abandonment many of us can relate to during our darkest moments. David's honesty with God in this psalm is raw and unfiltered, showing that bringing our deepest fears and doubts to God is okay.

On the other hand, there are psalms of thanksgiving and praise that reflect moments of profound gratitude and joy. Psalm 23:1-4 is a beautiful example, where David writes, "The Lord is my shepherd; I shall not want. He makes me lie down in green pastures. He leads me beside still waters. He restores my soul." These verses paint a picture of peace and contentment, starkly contrasting the anguish expressed in Psalm 22. This juxtaposition shows the full spectrum of human emotion, reminding us that our relationship with God encompasses both our highest highs and lowest lows.

David's psalms extend beyond expressions of distress to include poignant prayers of repentance. Consider Psalm 51:1-2, where David implores, "Have mercy on me, O God, in accordance with your unfailing love; in your vast compassion, erase my wrongdoings. Thoroughly wash away my guilt and purify me from my sin!" Composed in the aftermath of his transgression with Bathsheba, this psalm resonates with deep remorse, a longing for pardon, and a recognition of his faults.

David's earnest approach to seeking divine forgiveness exemplifies a path we might emulate when facing our ethical shortcomings. The historical and cultural context of the Psalms adds another layer of understanding to their significance. In ancient Israelite worship, psalms were used extensively in Temple services and synagogue worship. They were not just individual prayers but communal expressions of faith, sung and recited by the congregation. The musical and poetic structure of the psalms made them memorable and easy to incorporate into worship. This tradition has endured, with psalms continuing to play a central role in Jewish and Christian practices today.

The enduring influence of the Psalms on worship practices is undeniable. They offer a deeply personal yet universally relatable prayer language, enabling individuals and congregations alike to navigate the full spectrum of human emotion in the presence of the Divine. This remarkable adaptability ensures their perpetual relevance in liturgical settings as an invaluable tool for personal contemplation and communal devotion.

In today's world, the example set by the Psalms can guide us in our prayer and spiritual reflection practices. Modern spiritual practices that encourage emotional honesty often draw inspiration from the Psalms. Practices like journaling, where one writes down prayers and reflections, can help us articulate our emotions more clearly. Similarly, guided prayer sessions encouraging participants to express their feelings openly can foster a deeper connection with God. These practices emphasize that all emotions—joy, sorrow, anger, gratitude—are valid in prayer.

Expressing a full range of emotions in prayer is crucial for a healthy spiritual life. Holding back our true feelings can create a barrier between us and God. The Psalms teach us that God is big enough to handle our anger, doubts, and fears. Being honest in our prayers allows us to build a more authentic relationship with God that acknowledges the complexities of our human experience.

Reflect on how you express your emotions in prayer. Do you find it easy to be honest with God, or are there emotions you struggle to voice? Consider the steps to cultivate a more honest and open prayer life. This might involve setting aside time each day for reflective prayer, writing down your thoughts and feelings, or even speaking them out loud. The goal is to create a space where you feel free to bring all aspects of your life before God, knowing He listens and understands.

The Psalms offer a deeply human and profoundly spiritual model for prayer. David's expressions of lament, joy, and repentance teach us that emotional honesty is not only acceptable in prayer but essential. By following this example, we can develop a more prosperous, more authentic relationship with God that embraces the full spectrum of our human experience.

PROVERBS: PRACTICAL WISDOM FOR DAILY LIVING

See yourself as a member of a family gathering, and the elder of your family begins to share snippets of wisdom collected over a lifetime. This is what reading the Book of Proverbs feels like—a compilation of practical advice designed to guide us through life's complexities. Proverbs are structured as a collection of sayings and instructions attributed primarily to King Solomon. It addresses various aspects of daily life, offering practical wisdom that remains relevant today. One of the central themes in Proverbs is the contrast between wisdom and folly. Proverbs 9:1-6 presents wisdom as a woman who has built her house and prepared a feast, inviting the simple to gain insight. In contrast, Proverbs 9:13-18 depicts folly as a loud, ignorant woman who leads people astray. This vivid imagery emphasizes the importance of choosing wisdom over foolishness, highlighting the consequences of our decisions.

Proverbs offers timeless guidance on leading a life of ethical integrity and moral uprightness. Reflect on the wisdom of Proverbs 11:1-3, where it is written, "The Lord abhors dishonest scales, but accurate weights gain his favor. Pride leads to disgrace, whereas humility fosters wisdom. Their integrity steers the righteous, while deceit brings ruin to the deceitful." This passage highlights the virtues of honesty, humility, and integrity, urging us to live by higher, divine standards. It is a powerful reminder that authentic, ethical living transcends mere adherence to societal norms, challenging us to embody these virtues in every aspect of our lives. In a society often seduced by the allure of quick gains through dishonest means, the wisdom of Proverbs stands as a beacon, encouraging us to steadfastly maintain our commitment to our moral and ethical convictions.

Another significant theme in Proverbs is the importance of relationships and community. Proverbs 17:17 declares, "A friend loves at all times, and a brother is born for a time of adversity." This verse highlights the enduring nature of true friendship and the support provided by close relationships. The wisdom literature underscores the value of nurturing and maintaining strong bonds with others. It teaches us that relationships are not just social constructs but vital components of a fulfilling life. In a time where social media can create superficial connections, Proverbs reminds us of the depth and importance of genuine relationships.

Grasping Proverbs' historical and cultural context significantly enhances our understanding of its lessons. In the ancient Near East, wisdom literature, including Proverbs, was highly valued for imparting moral and practical guidance. These revered texts played a critical role in molding the societal moral code. For the ancient Israelites, wisdom was academic knowledge and a comprehensive lifestyle harmonizing with divine principles. Specifically, Proverbs was a cornerstone of education, providing young people with a guide to overcoming life's hurdles through divine wisdom. Applying the teachings of Proverbs to modern life can provide valuable insights into contemporary challenges and ethical dilemmas. For instance, maintaining integrity and avoiding deceit in the workplace can guide our professional conduct. Emphasizing loyalty, humility, and genuine friendship can help us build and sustain meaningful connections. Consider a scenario where you're tempted to cut corners at work to achieve quick success. The wisdom of Proverbs would advise against such actions, emphasizing the long-term benefits of honesty and integrity.

Seeking and practicing wisdom in daily decisions is crucial for navigating the complexities of modern life. Proverbs encourage us to be intentional about our choices, seek advice from trusted sources, and reflect on the consequences of our actions. In our fast-paced world, seeking wisdom can help us make more informed and ethical decisions. Whether it's managing finances, resolving conflicts, or pursuing personal growth, the practical wisdom offered in Proverbs can guide us toward a more fulfilling and balanced life.

Give thought to how you seek wisdom in your daily life. Do you turn to trusted mentors, spiritual texts, or personal reflection for guidance? Consider the sources you rely on and how they influence your decisions. What steps can you take to apply the practical teachings of Proverbs to your personal and professional life? Perhaps it involves setting aside time for reflection or consciously aligning your actions with ethical principles. The wisdom of Proverbs offers timeless guidance that can help us navigate the complexities of modern life with integrity and insight.

ECCLESIASTES: FINDING MEANING IN LIFE'S SEASONS

Imagine standing on the shoreline, gazing at the endless ocean as waves break upon the sand, each moment fleeting yet profound. This imagery captures the essence of Ecclesiastes, a book that probes the ephemeral nature of life through the reflections of the sage Qoheleth, often linked to King Solomon. Here, we are invited into a deep examination of life's purpose and the true meaning of existence.

Qoheleth opens his discourse with a profound declaration: "Vanity of vanities! All is vanity" (Ecclesiastes 1:2), laying the groundwork for contemplation on the fleeting and elusive quality of human endeavors and aspirations. This narrative depicts life as a quest as ephemeral as chasing the wind, urging readers to ponder over what genuinely endows our lives with significance.

Qoheleth's reflections on the search for meaning are particularly poignant. In Ecclesiastes 2:1-11, he describes his pursuit of pleasure, wisdom, and work, only to find that these pursuits ultimately lead to a sense of emptiness. He indulged in laughter, wine, and grand projects, building houses, planting vineyards, and amassing wealth. Yet, despite these accomplishments, he concludes, "Then I considered all that my hands had done and the toil I had spent in doing it, and again, all was vanity and a chasing after wind, and there was nothing to be gained under the sun" (Ecclesiastes 2:11). This realization highlights the limitations of earthly pursuits in providing lasting fulfillment.

One of the most well-known passages in Ecclesiastes is the reflection on the seasons of life, found in Ecclesiastes 3:1-8.

"For everything, there is a season, and a time for every matter under heaven: a time to be born, and a time to die; a time to plant, and a time to pluck up what is planted..." This poetic meditation captures the cyclical nature of existence, acknowledging that life is composed of various seasons, each with its purpose and significance. It reminds us that change is an inherent part of life, and finding meaning often involves recognizing and embracing these transitions.

Ecclesiastes starkly contrasts the rich mosaic of ancient wisdom literature, setting itself apart from texts like the Egyptian "Instruction of Amenemope" and the Mesopotamian "Epic of Gilgamesh." While these works provide valuable insights into moral and ethical living, Ecclesiastes further contemplates life's transient and often perplexing nature. Unlike the predominantly optimistic tone of Proverbs, it tackles the uncertainties and paradoxes of existence head-on. Its reflective and philosophical narrative invites readers to deeply explore what truly gives life meaning, marking a distinct departure from its contemporaries by questioning the permanence of worldly pursuits and achievements. This introspective journey through Ecclesiastes strikes a chord with contemporary audiences, navigating the seas of change and uncertainty that characterize modern life. The narrative finds a parallel in the life story of Viktor Frankl, a Holocaust survivor, and psychiatrist who, through his profound suffering, discovered that true meaning lies not in external success but in our response to life's challenges. His seminal work, "Man's Search for Meaning," underscores the importance of finding purpose, mirroring the existential inquiries at the heart of Ecclesiastes. Frankl's experiences and conclusions resonate with the book's message, affirming that the essence of life's significance is found amidst the ebbs and flows of our personal journeys.

Embracing the transient nature of life and finding joy in the present moment is a central lesson of Ecclesiastes. Rather than seeking fulfillment in material possessions or status, Qoheleth encourages us to find contentment in simple pleasures: enjoying food and drink, taking pleasure in our work, and cherishing relationships. This perspective invites us to live fully in the present, appreciating the beauty and significance of each moment.

Reflect on how you seek and find meaning in different seasons of your life. Do you anchor your sense of purpose in external achievements, or do you find contentment in the present moment? Consider the steps you can take to embrace the transient nature of life and find joy in the here and now. Perhaps it involves practicing mindfulness, cultivating gratitude, or savoring daily life's small pleasures. The wisdom of Ecclesiastes offers a timeless reminder that life's meaning is often found in the journey and the ebb and flow of its seasons.

CHAPTER NINE

MAJOR PROPHETS

You are a young adult living in a time of significant political instability. The threat of foreign invasion looms over your homeland, and uncertainty hangs thick in the air. In this chaotic environment, a voice emerges, offering a vision of hope and restoration. This voice belongs to Isaiah, one of the most significant prophets in Israel's history. His prophecies, recorded in the Book of Isaiah, span from warnings of impending judgment to promises of future redemption and peace.

ISAIAH'S VISION: HOPE AND RESTORATION

Isaiah's prophetic vision stands out for its depth and breadth, encompassing the themes of judgment, hope, and restoration. One of the most compelling aspects of Isaiah's message is his vision of the coming Messiah, found in Isaiah 9:6-7. "For to us a child is born, to us, a son is given, and the government will be on his shoulders. And he will be called Wonderful Counselor, Mighty God, Everlasting Father,

Prince of Peace." This passage paints a picture of a future leader who embodies divine attributes and will bring justice and righteousness. The Messiah's reign promises to establish an eternal kingdom, bringing peace and stability in stark contrast to the turmoil of Isaiah's time.

Another powerful vision in Isaiah's prophecies is the promise of a new heaven and earth, described in Isaiah 65:17-19. "See, I will create new heavens and a new earth. The former things will not be remembered, nor will they come to mind. But be glad and rejoice forever in what I will create, for I will create Jerusalem to be a delight and its people a joy." This vision offers a glimpse into a future where suffering and sorrow are replaced with joy and celebration. It speaks to the ultimate restoration and renewal of creation, a theme that resonates deeply with those seeking hope amidst despair.

Isaiah's imagery of the suffering servant, found in Isaiah 53:3-5, is another cornerstone of his prophetic message. "He was despised and rejected by humanity, a suffering man familiar with pain. Like one from whom people hide their faces, he was despised, and we held him in low esteem. Surely, he took up our pain and bore our suffering, yet we considered him punished by God, stricken by him, and afflicted. But he was pierced for our transgressions and crushed for our iniquities; the punishment that brought us peace was on him, and by his wounds, we are healed." This passage, often interpreted as a prophecy about Jesus Christ, portrays a figure who endures immense suffering to bring healing and redemption. The suffering servant's willingness to bear the pain and sins of others highlights the themes of sacrifice and divine love.

Grasping the full impact of Isaiah's prophecies necessitates a deep dive into his era's historical and cultural milieu. Isaiah's ministry took place during significant political and social upheaval. The Assyrian Empire was expanding its territory, constantly threatening the smaller kingdoms of Israel and Judah. The Israelite community was grappling with the fear of invasion and the destruction of their way of life. This fear was realized when the Northern Kingdom of Israel fell to the Assyrians in 722 BCE. The Southern Kingdom of Judah, where Isaiah primarily prophesied, faced challenges, including the looming threat of Babylonian conquest, eventually leading to the Babylonian exile.

Isaiah's prophecies addressed these dire circumstances, offering both warnings and hope. He called the people to repentance, urging them to turn away idolatry and injustice. At the same time, his visions of hope and restoration provided a counterbalance to the grim reality of their situation. The promise of a Messiah, the vision of a new creation, and the image of the suffering servant all pointed to a future where God's people would be restored and renewed.

Drawing lessons from Isaiah's vision can help us gain insights into our struggles with hope and restoration. Modern movements inspired by Isaiah's vision include the Civil Rights Movement, where leaders like Martin Luther King Jr. drew on biblical themes of justice and redemption to advocate for equality and social change. Isaiah reminds us that maintaining faith in God's promises is crucial during difficult times. It encourages us to look beyond our immediate circumstances and trust in a future where restoration and renewal are possible.

Reflect on your own experiences with hope and restoration. When have you experienced a sense of hope amidst despair? Perhaps it was during a challenging period in your personal life, such as a health crisis or a significant loss. How did you find hope and strength to persevere? Additionally, consider how you can hold onto the promise of restoration in your life. This could mean nurturing a practice of thankfulness or delving into the scriptures to remind oneself of God's assurances of restoration and hope.

Reflective Exercise

Take a few moments to journal when you felt a sense of hope amidst despair. What were the circumstances, and how did you find hope? Reflect on how you can continue nurturing this sense of hope and trust in God's promises. This exercise can help you identify sources of strength and inspiration to sustain you during challenging times.

JEREMIAH'S LAMENT: FAITH IN TIMES OF DESPAIR

You have just been tasked with conveying a message destined to provoke hostility. This was the reality for Jeremiah, who initially resisted his divine calling with a plea of inadequacy: "I do not know how to speak; I am too young" (Jeremiah 1:6). In response, God offered reassurance, vowing to guide his words and shield him from danger. Despite this divine assurance, Jeremiah's ministry was fraught with emotional and spiritual struggles. Known as the "weeping prophet," Jeremiah lamented over Jerusalem's impending doom, feeling the weight of his people's sins and the consequences they would face.

In Jeremiah 9:1, the prophet expresses a profound desire for endless mourning for his people, stating, "Oh, that my head were a spring of water and my eyes a fountain of tears! I would weep day and night for the slain of my people." This vivid imagery uncovers the depth of Jeremiah's anguish and his steadfast faith amid the gloom. A particularly striking moment is in Jeremiah 20:7-9, where he unveils his inner turmoil and distress. "You deceived me, Lord, and I was deceived; you overpowered me and prevailed. I am ridiculed all day long; everyone mocks me." Despite the scorn and personal suffering he encounters, Jeremiah remains inexorably drawn to his divine mission. "But if I say, 'I will not mention his word or speak any more in his name,' his word is in my heart like a fire, a fire shut up in my bones. I am weary of holding it in; indeed, I cannot." This passage poignantly illustrates the prophet's unwavering dedication, showcasing the intense internal struggle he endures for the sake of his calling.

Jeremiah's ministry occurred during a deep-rooted political instability and social turmoil in Judah. The kingdom was caught between powerful empires, with the Babylonians eventually conquering Jerusalem and leading many into exile. This conquest had devastating effects on the Jewish community, uprooting families and destroying their homeland. The Babylonians' destruction of Jerusalem and the Temple in 586 BCE marked the end of an era and the beginning of a challenging period of exile. The political instability of the time only added to the people's despair as they grappled with the loss of their city, their Temple, and their way of life.

Jeremiah's prophecies were delivered in this context of impending doom and eventual exile. His warnings about the consequences of sin and idolatry were often met with resistance and hostility. Yet, he remained steadfast in his mission. Judah's social and political conditions during this time were marked by fear, uncertainty, and a sense of impending disaster. The Jewish community struggled to understand why God would allow such devastation to occur, questioning their faith and their future. Jeremiah's laments and unwavering faith provided a voice for their grief and a beacon of hope amidst the darkness.

Drawing lessons from Jeremiah's experience, we can find valuable insights into maintaining faith during intense hardship. Modern individuals who have demonstrated faith amidst despair include figures like Nelson Mandela, who kept his vision for a better South Africa despite decades of imprisonment. Another example is writer Corrie ten Boom, who held onto her faith while enduring the horrors of a Nazi concentration camp. These individuals, like Jeremiah, faced overwhelming challenges yet found strength in their faith.

Honest lament is crucial in times of sorrow. Jeremiah's dialogues with God show that expressing frustration, anger, and deep sorrow is okay. These emotions do not signify a lack of faith but rather a profound engagement with it. Seeking God's presence in times of despair involves acknowledging our pain and turning to Him for comfort and guidance. This practice can be deeply healing, allowing us to confront our struggles while holding onto the hope of eventual restoration.

Reflect on your experiences with faith and despair. When have you experienced a season of despair? How did you maintain your faith? Perhaps it was during a difficult period, such as a significant loss or a personal crisis. Consider the steps to seek God's presence and comfort in times of sorrow. This might involve immersing yourself in scripture that speaks to your situation. By doing so, you can find strength and hope, even in the darkest of times.

EZEKIEL'S VALLEY OF DRY BONES: RENEWAL AND RESTORATION

Envision traveling to a desolate land encircled by the scattered remains of dry, brittle bones. This vivid imagery is drawn from Ezekiel's vision. Positioned in this valley of desolation, he is questioned by God, "Son of man, can these bones live?" (Ezekiel 37:3). Ezekiel, demonstrating unwavering faith in the divine, replies, "Sovereign Lord, you alone know." Following this, God commands Ezekiel to prophesy to these bones. As Ezekiel obeys, a miraculous transformation unfolds: the bones stir, align, and assemble into complete skeletons. What follows is the emergence of tendons, the overlay of flesh, and the encasement in skin— yet devoid of life. With Ezekiel's invocation of God's breath, these forms rise as a formidable army (Ezekiel 37:1-10).

This vision of dry bones coming to life is rich with symbolic meaning and theological significance. The dry bones represent the people of Israel, who felt hopeless and cut off during their exile in Babylon. The imagery of bones coming together, gaining flesh, and receiving breath symbolize the promise of renewal and restoration. God assured Ezekiel that He would put His Spirit in the people, bring them back to their land, and restore them as a nation (Ezekiel 37:11-14). This vision conveyed a powerful message: even in the bleakest circumstances, God's power can bring about renewal and restoration.

Understanding the historical and cultural backdrop of Ezekiel's prophecies is essential for grasping their profound impact. Amidst the Babylonian exile, the Jewish people endured severe hardships. They were displaced from their homeland and confronted with foreign customs and deities. The destruction of their sacred Temple in Jerusalem deepened their sense of divine abandonment. Within this bleak scenario, Ezekiel's prophetic visions emerged as a ray of hope. The metaphor of the valley of dry bones, in particular, symbolized not an end but a transformative beginning, assuring the exiles that God did not forsake them. This vision offered a promise of revival and renewal, indicating that their despair was merely a chapter in a larger narrative of redemption and restoration.

Prophetic visions like Ezekiel's were vital in offering hope and encouragement to the exiled community. These visions reminded the people of God's power and commitment to His promises. They provided a sense of purpose and direction, encouraging the exiles to hold onto their faith and look forward to a future restoration. Ezekiel's vision of the dry bones was particularly impactful because it addressed the deep hopelessness the exiles felt. It assured them that God could breathe new life into their seemingly lifeless situation.

Drawing lessons from Ezekiel's vision, we can apply the themes of spiritual renewal and restoration to modern challenges. Many communities today experience periods of spiritual dryness and disconnection. This can happen personally, where individuals feel distant from their faith, or at a communal level, where religious institutions struggle to remain relevant. Movements seeking spiritual renewal often draw inspiration from visions like Ezekiel's. For example, the revival movements in various religious traditions have focused on rekindling faith and restoring a sense of purpose and community.

The importance of prophetic vision and hope cannot be overstated in spiritual dryness. Prophetic voices, whether in religious or secular contexts, can inspire and mobilize communities. They remind us of the possibilities for renewal and encourage us to look beyond our current struggles. In Ezekiel's vision, the breath of God entering the bones symbolizes the life-giving power of the Spirit. This serves as a reminder that true renewal comes from a spiritual awakening and a reconnection with the divine.

Ponder your journey through spiritual drought and revival. Have there been moments when you've felt a profound disconnect from your spiritual essence? Reflect on the pathways you've sought for rejuvenation. Envision the actionable steps you might undertake to deeply anchor yourself in the assurance of divine renewal within your life. This could encompass dedicating consistent periods for spiritual disciplines or delving into enlightening scriptures and discourses.

Reflective Exercise

Take a few moments to journal when you felt spiritually dry or disconnected. What were the circumstances, and how did you seek renewal? Reflect on how you can continue to nurture your spiritual life and embrace the promise of restoration. This exercise can help you identify practices and resources to sustain you during spiritual dryness.

LAMENTATIONS: MOURNING AND HOPE

You stand before Jerusalem, once a vibrant city, which is now in ruins. The Temple, the heart of your spiritual and communal life, lies in ashes. This is the backdrop of the Book of Lamentations, a collection of mournful poems capturing the profound grief and suffering of the Jewish people after the Babylonian conquest in 586 BCE. The intensity of grief within these laments is deeply felt, each verse intricately crafting a landscape of loss and desolation. The initial lines immediately establish the mood: "How deserted lies the city, once teeming with life! How she resembles a widow, once esteemed among nations!" (Lamentations 1:1). By depicting the city as a widow in mourning, the narrative highlights the deep collective sorrow that its inhabitants endured.

The poetry of Lamentations, with verses of the initial chapters aligned with consecutive letters of the Hebrew alphabet, reflects a deep intertwining of artistic mastery and spiritual inquiry. This deliberate structure contrasts sharply with the chaos and heartache portrayed within its verses. Notably, the early sections of Lamentations 3 paint a picture of anguish and despair, navigating through a realm overshadowed by divine retribution. This vivid illustration lays bare a profound feeling of forsakenness and the harsh realities of exile, offering an intimate glance into the core themes of abandonment and endurance amidst adversity.

Yet, within this landscape of sorrow, Lamentations pivots towards hope in its third chapter. Verses 21-24 shine as a beacon of hope, reaffirming God's unwavering love and mercy: "Yet this I call to mind, and therefore I have hope: Because of the Lord's great love we are not consumed, for his compassions never fail. They are new every morning; great is your faithfulness." This moment of reflection reveals a profound theological truth—the resilience of God's love and mercy, even in the bleakest of times. It suggests that sorrow and hope are not mutually exclusive but can coexist, offering a foundation for healing and future renewal. Understanding the backdrop of Lamentations enriches its impact. The fall of Jerusalem and the subsequent destruction of the Temple by the Babylonians signify a pivotal, tragic moment for the Jewish people. Jerusalem, once a beacon of divine presence and safeguarding, was left in ruins, symbolizing not only a military defeat but a profound spiritual and emotional calamity. The obliteration of the Temple disrupted the sacred connection between the divine and the people, intensifying feelings of loss and desertion. The adversity of exile only deepened this anguish, challenging the survivors to preserve their identity and faith amid unfamiliar surroundings. The emotional toll of this period is vividly captured in the laments. The Jewish community grappled with questions of divine justice and faithfulness. Why had God allowed such devastation? How could they continue to worship without the Temple? These questions permeate the verses of Lamentations, reflecting the deep theological and existential crisis the exiled community faces. The poems serve as a means to process and express their collective grief, providing a space for mourning and reflection.

Drawing lessons from Lamentations, we can apply its themes to modern experiences of grief and the search for hope. In contemporary times, we face various forms of loss —whether it's the death of a loved one, the end of a significant relationship, or the loss of a job. The expression of grief and suffering in Lamentations resonates with our struggles, reminding us that it is okay to mourn and feel despair. Modern expressions of mourning, such as support groups, therapy, and memorial services, provide spaces for individuals to process their grief and find solace.

Acknowledging grief is a crucial step in finding hope. The turning point in Lamentations 3 emphasizes the importance of remembering God's faithfulness during times of loss. Seeking God's presence and comfort involves honest lament and a willingness to trust in His promises. This process can be deeply healing, allowing us to move from despair to hope. Reflect on your experiences with mourning and hope. When have you experienced a profound sense of loss? How did you mourn? Reflect on actionable steps to cultivate hope and reaffirm your trust in God's unwavering faithfulness amidst mourning. Turning to prayer and immersing yourself in scriptures that speak to your circumstances can profoundly influence navigating these moments.

Reflective Exercise:

Take a moment to journal about a time when you experienced a profound sense of loss. What were the circumstances, and how did you mourn? Reflect on how you can continue to find hope and trust in God's faithfulness during mourning. This exercise can help you identify practices and resources to provide comfort and strength during difficult times.

Each subchapter in Chapter 9 explores significant themes of mourning, hope, faith, and restoration, offering valuable insights for navigating life's challenges. As we transition to the next chapter, we will continue to explore the profound lessons found in the Minor Prophets, delving into their messages of justice, mercy, and divine promise.

CHAPTER TEN

MINOR PROPHETS

Imagine a marriage doomed from the start. You're standing at the altar, knowing that betrayal will come, not just once, but repeatedly. This was the reality for Hosea, a prophet called to marry Gomer, an adulterous woman. It's a story that seems more fitting for a dramatic novel than a sacred text. Yet, Hosea's marriage was a powerful metaphor for God's relationship with Israel. This narrative in the Book of Hosea offers profound insights into love, faithfulness, and redemption.

HOSEA'S FAITHFULNESS: LOVE AND REDEMPTION

When God instructed Hosea to marry Gomer, a woman notorious for lacking fidelity, it marked a significant shift in Hosea's life. This directive, as outlined in Hosea 1:2-3, transcended a mere personal ordeal, serving instead as a profound emblematic act. The union between Hosea and Gomer was a reflective parallel of the divine covenant between God and Israel, a nation that had strayed in pursuit of other deities. Hosea's steadfast loyalty amidst Gomer's betrayals exemplified the depth of God's enduring devotion to His people. This union, marred by heartache, served as a poignant metaphor for the spiritual waywardness of Israel and the boundless love of God.

The names of Hosea and Gomer's children further underscored this symbolic relationship. Their first child was named Jezreel, a reference to the site of a massacre and a symbol of impending judgment on Israel (Hosea 1:4-5). Their daughter, Lo-Ruhamah, meaning "No Mercy," indicated that God would no longer show mercy to Israel because of their persistent unfaithfulness (Hosea 1:6). Lastly, their son, Lo-Ammi, meaning "Not My People," reflected the broken relationship between God and Israel (Hosea 1:9). These names were not mere labels but prophetic declarations of Israel's spiritual state and the consequences of their actions.

Gomer's continued infidelity and Hosea's unwavering faithfulness are potent metaphors for divine love and forgiveness. Despite Gomer's repeated betrayals, Hosea was instructed by God to bring her back and love her again (Hosea 3:1-3). This act of reclaiming Gomer symbolized God's desire to restore His relationship with Israel despite their waywardness. It vividly portrays God's long-suffering patience and willingness to forgive and redeem. During Hosea's era, the fabric of Israelite society in the Northern Kingdom was deeply marred by idol worship and a widespread departure from spiritual fidelity. The populace's devotion to Baal and various other deities not only represented a departure from their faith but also a profound violation of the sacred covenant with God. Compounded by this spiritual crisis were the socio-political upheavals of the time. Threats from formidable forces like the Assyrian Empire contributed to a climate of political fragility and societal anxiety. In this volatile context, Hosea's life choices, particularly his marriage to Gomer, stood as a bold indictment against the pervasive spiritual corruption and moral decline, signaling a call back to covenant faithfulness.

Reflecting on Hosea's narrative, we can draw valuable lessons on love, faithfulness, and redemption. Maintaining love and devotion can be challenging in our modern relationships, especially when faced with betrayal and disappointment. However, Hosea's story reminds us of the importance of unconditional love and forgiveness. Just as Hosea was called to love Gomer despite her flaws, we are called to extend grace and compassion in our relationships. This doesn't mean ignoring wrongdoing but choosing to forgive and seek reconciliation.

Consider the examples of modern relationships that exemplify faithfulness and redemption. Couples who have weathered storms of infidelity and emerged stronger often cite forgiveness and open communication as key factors in their healing. The story of Hosea and Gomer encourages us to practice these virtues in our own lives. Reflect on a time when you experienced or witnessed unconditional love and faithfulness. How did it impact you? What steps can you take to practice love and forgiveness in your relationships?

Reflective Exercise: Journaling

Take a moment to journal about a relationship in which you have shown or received deep loyalty and forgiveness. Reflect on the actions and attitudes that contributed to healing and strengthening that bond. Consider practical steps to nurture love and faithfulness in your current relationships. This exercise can help you internalize the lessons from Hosea's story and apply them to your own life.

AMOS' JUSTICE: SOCIAL JUSTICE AND FAITH

Imagine residing in a society characterized by escalating wealth disparities, where affluence accumulates at the top while the less fortunate struggle for survival. The prophet Amos found himself in such a world. He delivered a powerful message reverberating through the ages, condemning social inequalities and calling for justice and righteousness. Amos was particularly critical of Israel's complacency and luxury, as described in Amos 6:1-6. The affluent Israelites lounged on ivory beds, indulging in feasts and listening to music, while the poor languished in need. This lifestyle of excess and indifference starkly contrasted with the values of justice and humility God desired.

"Let justice roll on like a river, righteousness like a never-failing stream," Amos proclaimed in Amos 5:24. This vivid imagery wasn't just poetic; it was a clarion call for the people to live out their faith through actions of justice. Amos envisioned a society where justice flowed continuously, unimpeded by barriers of greed and corruption. He saw righteousness as a constant, life-giving force, much like a perennial stream that nourishes and sustains. This call for justice was a direct challenge to the hollow rituals and worship practices that had become prevalent. Amos emphasized that true worship was inseparable from righteous living and social justice.

One of the most striking images in Amos' prophecies is the vision of the plumb line, found in Amos 7:7-9. God showed Amos a plumb line, a tool used by builders to ensure walls were straight. This vision symbolized God's standard of righteousness and justice. Just as a plumb line reveals crooked walls, God's standard exposed the moral decay and injustice in Israel. The message was clear: Israel had failed to measure up, and judgment was imminent. This vision was a powerful reminder that God's expectations for justice and righteousness were non-negotiable. It underscored the importance of aligning one's life with divine standards.

To understand the weight of Amos' message, it's crucial to consider the socio-economic conditions of Israel during his time. The nation experienced economic prosperity, but this wealth was concentrated in the hands of a few. The poor were exploited, and the gap between the rich and the needy widened. Landowners and merchants engaged in deceitful practices, further impoverishing the vulnerable. Amos condemned this exploitation, warning that such injustices would lead to divine retribution. He also criticized the religious hypocrisy of those who performed rituals and sacrifices while ignoring the plight of the oppressed. This disconnect between faith and practice was a central theme in Amos' prophecies.

Reflecting on Amos' message, we see parallels to modern social inequality and ethical living issues. Today, movements advocating for social justice echo Amos' call for righteousness. Organizations and activists work tirelessly to address systemic inequalities, from economic disparities to racial injustices. They remind us that faith must be active in efforts to create a just and equitable society. The importance of integrating faith with actions of justice and righteousness cannot be overstated. It's about living out our beliefs in tangible ways, ensuring that our worship aligns with our treatment of others.

Consider how you respond to issues of social injustice in your community. Do you stay silent, or do you take action? Reflect on your responsibilities towards social justice and ethical living. What steps can you take to align your faith with actions of justice and righteousness? Maybe it's volunteering with organizations supporting the marginalized, advocating for policy changes, or treating everyone with dignity and respect. These actions, big or small, contribute to the continuous flow of justice that Amos envisioned.

Reflective Exercise: Checklist for Social Justice

1. Identify local organizations advocating for social justice and consider how you can support them.
2. Reflect on your daily interactions and ensure they reflect dignity and respect for all individuals.
3. Advocate for policies that address systemic inequalities in your community.
4. Engage in continuous learning about social justice issues to stay informed and proactive.

MICAH'S CALL: WALKING HUMBLY WITH GOD

Micah's call to "do justice, love kindness, and walk humbly with God" encapsulates the essence of his prophetic message. This directive, found in Micah 6:8, is a timeless guide for personal conduct. It's a straightforward yet profound call to action that resonates deeply. Micah's message came at a time of significant moral and social decay in Judah. The prophets were often seen as the people's moral compass, and Micah was no exception. He condemned the corrupt leaders and false prophets who exploited their positions for personal gain. In Micah 3:1-5, he didn't mince words, denouncing those who "tear the skin from my people and the flesh from their bones." These leaders were supposed to protect and serve, but instead, they perpetuated injustice and oppression. Micah's fierce denunciation of their actions highlighted the gap between the leaders' behavior and God's expectations for justice and righteousness.

Amidst this condemnation, Micah offered hope by prophesying about a future ruler from Bethlehem. This prophecy, found in Micah 5:2-4, foretold the coming of a leader who would shepherd the people with strength and majesty. This ruler would bring peace and restoration, standing in stark contrast to the corrupt leaders of Micah's time. The promise of a future leader from a humble town like Bethlehem emphasized the importance of humility in leadership. It was a reminder that authentic leadership is not about power and exploitation but about serving and guiding with integrity and compassion.

To fully appreciate Micah's message, it's essential to understand the historical and cultural context of his prophecies. Micah prophesied during a period of political upheaval and social corruption in Judah. The impending threat of the Assyrian invasion added to the sense of urgency in his message. The leaders of Judah were corrupt, exploiting the poor and vulnerable while ignoring the cries for justice. This corruption was a betrayal of the people's trust and a direct violation of the covenantal relationship between God and

His people. The social and political conditions of Judah were dire, with the Assyrian threat looming large. This external pressure further exposed the internal moral decay, making Micah's call for justice, kindness, and humility even more poignant.

Applying Micah's call to modern challenges, we see the enduring relevance of his message. Today, we face our own set of ethical dilemmas and social injustices. Micah's directive to "do justice" calls us to actively engage in creating a fair and equitable society. It challenges us to advocate for the marginalized and fight against systemic inequalities. Examples of modern individuals who exemplify this commitment to justice include figures.

Examples of modern individuals who embody this commitment to justice include leaders and activists renowned for their dedication to human rights and equality. Their lives inspire us to weave justice into the fabric of our daily existence, ensuring our faith manifests in actions that foster a fair and equitable society, who have dedicated their lives to fighting for human rights and equality. Their actions inspire us to integrate justice into our daily lives, ensuring that our faith is reflected in our efforts to create a just society.

"Loving kindness" goes beyond mere acts of charity; it involves cultivating a genuine spirit of compassion and empathy. It's about treating others with respect and understanding and recognizing their inherent dignity. This kindness should permeate our daily interactions, influencing how we treat friends, family, and strangers. Practicing kindness in our interactions can transform relationships and communities, fostering a culture of mutual respect and support.

"Walking humbly with God" is perhaps the most challenging aspect of Micah's call. It requires a deep sense of humility, recognizing our limitations, and seeking guidance from a higher power. Humility involves letting go of pride and ego and acknowledging that we are not the center of the universe. It's about being teachable and open to growth, understanding that true wisdom comes from walking in alignment with God's will. Modern examples of humility can be seen in individuals who quietly serve others without seeking recognition, embodying the spirit of humble service.

Reflect on how you practice justice, kindness, and humility daily. Are there areas where you can improve? Consider the steps you can take to walk more humbly with God. This might involve regular self-reflection, seeking feedback from trusted friends, or dedicating time to spiritual practices that nurture humility. Integrating these values into our lives allows us to live out Micah's call and contribute to a more just, kind, and humble world.

MALACHI'S PROMISE: FAITHFULNESS AND FULFILLMENT

Imagine living when your community is trying to rebuild and find its footing after exile and hardship. This was the reality for the people of post-exilic Judah; in this context, Malachi spoke his prophetic words. Malachi's message centered on faithfulness and the promise of future fulfillment, urging the people to return to God and honor Him properly. In Malachi 3:7-12, the prophet calls the people to return to God, emphasizing that their faithfulness would be met with divine blessing. "Return to me, and I will return to you," says the Lord Almighty. This promise calls for spiritual renewal and a guarantee of tangible blessings, such as fruitful harvests and protection from pests. The people's faithfulness to God would result in His faithfulness to them, creating a reciprocal relationship rooted in trust and obedience.

One of the most striking elements of Malachi's prophecy is the promise of a coming messenger and the Day of the Lord, as described in Malachi 3:1-2. This messenger would prepare the way for the Lord, refining and purifying the people like a refiner's fire and a launderer's soap. The imagery here is vivid and powerful, suggesting a thorough cleansing and preparation for the divine presence. While often associated with judgment, the Day of the Lord also promises renewal and restoration. For the people of Judah, this prophecy was a reminder of God's active role in their history and His ongoing commitment to their future.

Malachi also emphasized the importance of honoring God through proper worship and offerings. In Malachi 1:6-8, he rebukes the people for offering blemished sacrifices, highlighting their disregard for God's holiness. "When you offer blind animals for sacrifice, is that not wrong?" Malachi's words challenge the people to examine their worship quality and attitude towards God. According to Malachi, proper worship is not just about following rituals but giving God the honor He deserves. This means offering the best of what we have, not the leftovers. It's a call to genuine devotion and reverence.

Grasping the depth of Malachi's prophecies requires an immersion into Judah's historical and cultural backdrop after their return from exile. This period was marked by the community's efforts to reconstruct their identity and faith amidst the challenges of re-establishing their homeland. The rebuilding of the Temple initially rekindled a spiritual awakening. Yet, as time passed, enthusiasm dimmed, leading to a decline in religious fervor and moral standards. Malachi's messages served as a crucial call to action, pressing the people to rejuvenate their covenant with God and restore their worship's essence and integrity.

Having been re-erected, the Temple stood as a physical manifestation of God's presence among them and a central place for reinvigorating communal worship and faithfulness. After returning from Babylonian exile, the people faced the daunting task of rebuilding their lives and community. The Temple had been rebuilt, but the initial enthusiasm had waned, leading to religious and moral laxity. The people's worship had become perfunctory, and their commitment to God had weakened. Malachi's message was a wake-up call, urging them to renew their covenant relationship with God and re-establish proper worship practices. As the center of their religious life, the Temple played a crucial role in this renewal, serving as a tangible symbol of God's presence and a focal point for communal worship.

Applying Malachi's message to modern challenges, we see the importance of remaining faithful and hopeful for future fulfillment. In our fast-paced, often chaotic lives, it's easy to let our spiritual practices become routine or to neglect them altogether. Yet, Malachi's call to faithfulness reminds us that our relationship with God requires ongoing effort and attention. Examples of modern individuals and communities who maintain faithfulness despite challenges can be found in various religious traditions. Think of communities that gather regularly for prayer, service, and support despite external pressures. Their actions demonstrate the power of collective commitment to faith.

Hopeful anticipation and preparation for future fulfillment are critical themes in Malachi's message. Just as the people of Judah were called to prepare for the coming of the Lord, we are invited to live in a state of readiness, looking forward to fulfilling God's promises. This involves passive waiting and active engagement in practices that align us with God's will. It means living with purpose and expectation, knowing our faithfulness will be rewarded.

Reflect on how you remain faithful in your relationship with God. Are there areas where your devotion has become routine? Consider the steps to prepare for and anticipate God's future fulfillment in your life. This might involve deepening your prayer life or finding new ways to serve others. By actively nurturing your faith, you can create a life reflecting the promises and hope in Malachi's prophecies.

CHAPTER ELEVEN

NEW TESTAMENT BEGINNINGS

Imagine living in a small, unremarkable village, where your days are filled with the routine tasks of home and family life, interspersed with fleeting dreams of a life beyond the familiar. One serene evening, as the day gives way to night, a remarkable figure appears before you—the angel Gabriel. This visitation transcends the boundaries of the imaginable, heralding a message that promises to transform your path and alter the course of history itself. This is the extraordinary summons of Mary of Nazareth, chosen for a role unparalleled in the annals of time. The Annunciation to Mary is a powerful testament to faith in that which lies beyond our sight. The angel Gabriel's visit to Mary is one of the most profound moments in the New Testament. In Luke 1:26-33, Gabriel greets Mary with the words, "Greetings, you who are highly favored! The Lord is with you." It's hard to fathom the mixture of emotions Mary must have felt— fear, confusion, awe. Gabriel's message is astonishing: Mary, a virgin, will conceive a child who will be called the Son of the Most High. This child will inherit the throne of David, and his kingdom will never end. Gabriel's announcement is not just about a birth; it's a proclamation of a divine plan that has unfolded since the beginning.

Mary's initial reaction, as recorded in Luke 1:34, is understandable. "How will this be," Mary asks, "since I am a virgin?" Her question is practical, rooted in the realities of her situation. Yet, Gabriel reassures her that the Holy Spirit will come upon her, and the power of the Most High will overshadow her. The child born will be holy and called the Son of God. Though still mysterious, this explanation provides Mary with the assurance that what seems impossible is indeed possible with God.

What follows is a testament to Mary's remarkable faith and trust. In Luke 1:38, Mary responds, "I am the Lord's servant. May your word to me be fulfilled." Her acceptance is not a passive resignation but an active embrace of God's will. Mary's declaration of faith in the unseen is a powerful example of trust and surrender to God's plan despite the uncertainties and potential consequences.

Understanding Mary's situation's historical and cultural context adds depth to her story. In first-century Judea, women held a subordinate status in society. They were often seen through the lens of their roles as daughters, wives, and mothers. Being betrothed to Joseph, Mary was in a legally binding agreement more significant than modern engagements. Betrothal meant that Mary and Joseph had exchanged consent to marry. Still, they had not yet begun living together or having sexual relations. The announcement of her pregnancy could have brought severe consequences, including public disgrace and even the risk of being stoned for adultery. Yet, Mary's faith led her to accept this divine role with grace and courage.

Mary's story resonates deeply with modern challenges of faith and trust in the unseen. Her willingness to embrace God's plan, despite societal pressures and personal risks, offers timeless lessons. Consider modern individuals who have demonstrated similar faith in uncertain circumstances. Think of people like Mother Teresa, who left the comfort of her convent to serve the poorest of the poor in Calcutta; this example shows that faith in the unseen can lead to extraordinary outcomes.

Trusting in God's plans, especially when they defy logic or societal norms, requires immense courage. Mary's example encourages us to have faith even when we cannot see the whole picture. Reflect on your experiences when you were called to trust God's plans despite uncertainty. Perhaps it was a career change that didn't make sense then or a move to a new city where everything was unfamiliar. What gave you the strength to take that leap of faith? How did you navigate the pressures and doubts that inevitably arose?

To deepen your faith amidst societal challenges, incorporate daily rituals that bolster your reliance on God. Prayer, meditation, and scripture study serve as essential sources of spiritual sustenance, anchoring you in your faith journey. Participating in a faith-based community can further enrich this experience, providing support and accountability. Reflect upon moments of doubt or uncertainty in your life and consider how you navigated these times. Identifying steps to fortify your trust in God's overarching plan is crucial, even when it appears indistinct or daunting. The narrative of Mary illustrates that, through steadfast faith, we are empowered to accept the unseen and partake in the unfolding of God's remarkable plans.

JOHN THE BAPTIST: PREPARING THE WAY

It is a time when the voice of prophecy had been silent for nearly four hundred years. Suddenly, a man emerges from the wilderness, clothed in camel's hair and eating locusts and wild honey. This man is John the Baptist, a figure whose very appearance and lifestyle set him apart from the societal norms of the day. His message is clear and urgent: "Repent, for the kingdom of heaven is near" (Matthew 3:1-2). John's call to repentance is a moral exhortation and a profound spiritual awakening. He baptizes those who repent, symbolizing their purification and readiness for the coming Messiah.

The wilderness setting of John's ministry is significant. It evokes memories of Israel's time in the wilderness, a period of testing and renewal. In Matthew 3:3-4, John is described as "a voice of one calling in the wilderness, 'Prepare the way for the Lord, make straight paths for him.'" The wilderness is not just a backdrop but a place of spiritual significance. It represents a return to basics, a stripping away of the distractions and corruptions of society. John's ascetic lifestyle underscores his message of repentance and preparation. His diet of locusts and wild honey and his simple attire emphasize purity and a focus on spiritual rather than material wealth.

John's message about the coming Messiah is another cornerstone of his ministry. In John 1:26-27, he speaks of someone coming after him, "the straps of whose sandals I am not worthy to untie." This statement reflects John's profound humility and recognition of the Messiah's supreme authority. John's role is to prepare the people for the transformative message and ministry of Jesus. He is a transitional figure, linking the Old Testament prophets with the advent of the New Testament savior.

Understanding the historical and cultural context of John the Baptist's role helps us appreciate the depth of his mission. In first-century Judaism, ritual purification was a common practice. As a form of ritual washing, baptism symbolized repentance and readiness to enter a new way of life. Jewish eschatological expectations were high at this time. Many Jews anticipated a Messiah who would liberate them from Roman rule and restore Israel's former glory. John's call for repentance and his announcement of the coming kingdom would have resonated deeply with these expectations.

John's ministry reminds us of the importance of preparation and repentance in our spiritual lives. In a world filled with distractions and moral ambiguities, John's call to turn away from sin and prepare for God's presence remains profoundly relevant. Modern spiritual practices like fasting, meditation, and retreats can help us remove the noise and focus on our relationship with God. These practices help us prepare our hearts and minds to experience God's presence fully.

Recognizing and turning away from sin is crucial to personal spiritual growth. It's not just about feeling sorry for our wrongdoings but about consciously changing our behavior and aligning our lives with God's will. This process of repentance and renewal can be challenging, but it's essential for deepening our faith. Modern examples of repentance can be seen in the stories of individuals who have turned their lives around after struggling with addiction, crime, or other destructive behaviors. Their journeys show us that true repentance leads to profound transformation and a renewed sense of purpose.

Reflect on your own experiences with spiritual preparation and repentance. How do you prepare yourself spiritually for experiencing God's presence? Perhaps it's through daily prayer, reading scripture, or spending time in nature. What steps can you take to practice repentance and renewal in your life? Maybe it involves seeking forgiveness from someone you've wronged or committing to change a specific behavior. Take a moment to consider these questions and how they apply to your spiritual journey.

JESUS' BAPTISM: IDENTITY AND MISSION

Imagine standing at the edge of the Jordan River, surrounded by a crowd of people who have come to be baptized by John. The air is thick with anticipation and the murmur of voices. Suddenly, a man steps forward, and a hush falls over the crowd as he approaches John. This man is Jesus, and what happens next will mark the beginning of his public ministry and affirm his divine identity and mission. In Matthew 3:13-15, Jesus comes to John to be baptized, but John initially resists, saying, "I need to be baptized by you, and do you come to me?" Jesus replies, "Let it be so now; it is proper for us to do this to fulfill all righteousness." With this, John consents, and Jesus is baptized in the Jordan River.

The significance of Jesus' baptism is profound. It is not merely a ritual of purification but a pivotal moment that marks the start of his mission. As Jesus rises from the water, the heavens open, and the Spirit of God descends like a dove to rest upon him. Then, a voice from heaven declares, "This is my Son, whom I love; with him I am well pleased" (Matthew 3:16-17). This divine affirmation publicly identifies Jesus as the Son of God and sets the stage for his ministry. The moment the Holy Spirit descends like a dove upon Jesus marks a significant affirmation of his divine mission, anointing him for the journey ahead. Simultaneously, the voice from heaven declaring, "This is my Son, whom I love; with him, I am well pleased," unequivocally establishes Jesus' divine filiation. This profound event not only underscores the core of Jesus' identity but also signifies God's endorsement of his earthly mission.

To fully grasp the significance of Jesus' baptism, it's essential to delve into the historical and cultural backdrop of baptism within the Jewish tradition. Traditionally, baptism served as a purification ritual, a symbolic act of repentance, and a means to cleanse oneself of sins. However, with the advent of early Christianity, baptism transcended its initial purpose. It evolved into a profound emblem of rebirth, marking an individual's entrance into the Christian faith and serving as a profound declaration of one's belief. In the era Jesus lived, choosing to be baptized was deeply rooted in humility and compliance, notably for someone perceived as sinless.

Consequently, Jesus undergoing baptism was emblematic of his solidarity with humankind, presaging his imminent role as the redeemer of sins. One of the powerful lessons we can draw from Jesus' baptism is the importance of understanding and embracing our identity and mission. Modern-day examples of individuals who have embraced their divine calling can be incredibly inspiring. Consider figures like Martin Luther King Jr., who felt called to lead a movement for civil rights, or Mother Teresa, who dedicated her life to serving the poorest of the poor. Despite their challenges, these individuals recognized and pursued their mission with unwavering dedication. Their lives reflect the essence of Jesus' baptism—embracing one's identity and mission with faith and courage.

Recognizing and affirming one's divine calling involves introspection and spiritual discernment. It means listening for God's voice in our lives and being open to the guidance of the Holy Spirit. It also requires a willingness to step out in faith, even when the path ahead is uncertain. This process can be challenging, especially in a world that often values tangible achievements over spiritual growth. However, understanding and fulfilling our divine calling brings a sense of purpose and alignment with God's life plan.

Reflect on how you understand your identity and mission in the context of your faith. Have there been moments when you felt a strong sense of calling or purpose? How did you respond? Perhaps it was a nudge to help someone in need, a career shift that aligned with your values, or a personal project that felt deeply meaningful. What steps can you take to affirm and fulfill your divine calling? This might involve seeking guidance from a mentor or taking actions that align with your sense of purpose. Embracing your identity and mission, just as Jesus did, can lead to a life of profound impact and fulfillment.

JESUS' TEMPTATION: OVERCOMING LIFE'S TRIALS

Venture into the stark wilderness, under the unyielding glare of the sun, where life seems almost absent. Here, hunger gnaws at your strength, leaving you faint and weary. Into this unforgiving landscape steps Jesus, marking the onset of His earthly ministry. Following His baptism and led by the Spirit, He embarks on a forty-day sojourn of fasting and prayer, a time chronicled in Matthew 4:1-2. This ordeal transcends physical survival, a profound spiritual odyssey preparing Him for future challenges. The temptations He encounters are intricately linked to His very essence and the monumental task He is to undertake.

The first temptation came when Satan challenged Jesus to turn stones into bread to satisfy his hunger (Matthew 4:3). Jesus responded by quoting scripture: "Man shall not live on bread alone, but on every word that comes from the mouth of God" (Matthew 4:4). This response emphasized the importance of spiritual nourishment over physical needs. Satan then took Jesus to the pinnacle of the temple and urged him to throw himself down, arguing that God's angels would save him (Matthew 4:5-6). Jesus countered with another scripture: "Do not put the Lord your God to the test" (Matthew 4:7). This highlighted the necessity of trusting God without demanding proof of His care. Finally, Satan offered Jesus all the kingdoms of the world in exchange for worship (Matthew 4:8-9). Jesus firmly rejected this, declaring, "Worship the Lord your God, and serve him only" (Matthew 4:10). Each temptation and response underscored Jesus' unwavering commitment to God's will and reliance on scripture for guidance.

The wilderness experience is rich in symbolism. In the Bible, the wilderness often represents a place of trial and testing. The Israelites wandered in the wilderness for forty years, facing trials that tested their faith and obedience. For Jesus, the wilderness was a setting for proving his readiness for the mission ahead. It was where he could confront and overcome humanity's fundamental temptations: the lure of materialism, the desire for sensationalism, and the pursuit of power. The role of scriptural knowledge in resisting these temptations cannot be overstated. Jesus' responses to Satan were not just clever retorts; they were deeply rooted in the teachings of the Hebrew Scriptures, which provided a foundation for his resistance.

The lessons from Jesus' temptation are incredibly relevant in our modern context. We all face trials and temptations in various forms. Whether it's the temptation to prioritize work over family, the allure of material wealth, or the desire for instant gratification, these challenges test our character and faith. Consider the stories of individuals who have faced significant trials and emerged stronger. Think of people like Viktor Frankl, who survived the horrors of concentration camps and found meaning in suffering, or J.K. Rowling, who overcame personal and financial struggles to become a celebrated author. Like Jesus, their stories remind us that overcoming life's trials often involves deep spiritual discipline and resilience.

Spiritual discipline plays a crucial role in overcoming challenges. Relying on scripture, as Jesus did, offers a powerful tool for navigating life's difficulties. It provides wisdom, comfort, and guidance, helping us stay grounded in our faith. Reflect on your own experiences with trials and temptations.

When have you faced significant challenges that tested your resolve? How did you respond? Consider the steps to rely more on scripture and spiritual discipline in overcoming your challenges. Perhaps it involves setting aside time each day for quiet reflection or joining a study group to deepen your understanding of sacred texts. These practices can help you build a solid spiritual foundation, enabling you to face life's trials with confidence and faith.

As we explore the New Testament beginnings, the stories of faith, preparation, baptism, and temptation offer profound insights. They show us that spiritual growth involves embracing our identity, preparing our hearts, and trusting God's plan. These narratives guide us through the complexities of faith, encouraging us to live with purpose and resilience.

CHAPTER TWELVE
ACTS OF THE APOSTLES

Amid the ancient, revered walls of Jerusalem, you stand alone with the apostles in a room. The air is thick with a mix of eager anticipation and lingering doubt. After Jesus ascended to heaven, He left behind a promise of the Holy Spirit's imminent arrival to empower you for the mission ahead. As time blurs, a significant event unfolds. This day, known as Pentecost, marks a pivotal moment in Christian history. It transforms a small group of faithful followers into a powerful force set to change the world. Pentecost: Empowerment by the Holy Spirit On the day of Pentecost, the apostles were gathered together in one place, a scene that would soon be filled with divine energy. A sound like a rushing wind filled the room as they sat, perhaps praying or discussing their next steps. It wasn't just a gentle breeze but something powerful and overwhelming, shaking the very foundations of their gathering place (Acts 2:1-2). This was no ordinary wind; it was the breath of God, filling them with a sense of awe and expectation.

Then, something even more astonishing happened. Tongues of fire appeared and rested on each of them. These weren't literal flames but a divine manifestation, symbolizing the Holy Spirit's presence and empowerment (Acts 2:3-4). Imagine the scene: small flames hovering over their heads, a visible sign of an invisible power. This event wasn't just spectacular; it was deeply symbolic. Fire in the Hebrew scriptures often represents God's presence, as seen in the burning bush with Moses or the fire on Mount Sinai. This divine fire rested not on a place but on people, signifying that God's temple was now within the community of believers.

As the Holy Spirit descended, the apostles began to speak in various languages. This event wasn't unintelligible sounds but clear, purposeful communication that broke through language barriers, connecting with the diverse crowd of Jews who had gathered in Jerusalem to observe Shavuot. Known also as the Feast of Weeks, Shavuot was a significant Jewish harvest festival, drawing people from across the globe to the city. This miraculous ability to speak in various tongues was by divine design, enabling the apostles to spread the gospel beyond cultural and linguistic barriers, creating a profound sense of unity and shared spiritual experience among those present (Acts 2:3-4). Peter rose to address the crowd with newfound courage from the Holy Spirit. He proclaimed that the events unfolding before them fulfilled long-held prophecies, heralding Jesus as the awaited Messiah. The impact of Peter's sermon was so profound that about 3,000 individuals were moved to convert and be baptized that day (Acts 2:14, 41). Picture the scene: a multitude of people from varied backgrounds, converging in faith and community, ignited by a renewed belief. This remarkable day signaled the establishment of the Church, a fellowship invigorated by the Holy Spirit to fulfill the mission set forth by Jesus.

The significance of Pentecost extends beyond this single event. Historically, Pentecost was a Jewish festival celebrating the first fruits of the harvest and commemorating the giving of the Law on Mount Sinai. With the outpouring of the Holy Spirit, Pentecost took on a new meaning, symbolizing the beginning of a spiritual harvest and the formation of a new covenant community (SOURCE 1). Theologically, it marked the transition from an agricultural celebration to a celebration of divine empowerment, where the Holy Spirit equipped believers for their mission.

For today's faithful, the story of Pentecost provides deep insights into spiritual empowerment and the calling to carry out our missions. Many people today experience the Holy Spirit in diverse and powerful ways. Take, for example, the stories of individuals who feel a sudden urge to help others, leading to life-changing acts of kindness and service. Or consider those who experience a deep sense of peace and clarity during prayer, guided by a force beyond themselves. These experiences echo the empowerment of the apostles, reminding us that the Holy Spirit continues to work in our lives today.

Recognizing and utilizing spiritual gifts is crucial for the health and growth of faith communities. Just as the apostles used their gifts to spread the gospel, we are called to identify and use our spiritual gifts. Whether teaching, healing, hospitality, or administration, each gift plays a vital role in building the community and fulfilling God's mission. Understanding that these gifts are not for personal glory but for the common good encourages us to serve selflessly and support one another.

Take a moment to reflect on your own experiences with the Holy Spirit. When have you felt empowered by a force beyond yourself? Perhaps it was a moment of clarity during a difficult decision, a sense of peace amidst chaos, or an overwhelming urge to help someone in need. These experiences are not coincidences but manifestations of the Holy Spirit working in your life. How can you recognize and use your spiritual gifts to serve your community? Identifying your gifts may require prayer, self-reflection, and feedback from trusted friends. Once identified, consider how you can use these gifts in your faith community, whether through formal ministry roles or everyday acts of kindness and support.

PAUL'S CONVERSION: TRANSFORMATION AND MISSION

Envision yourself as Saul of Tarsus, a Pharisee distinguished by his fervent pursuit of Christians. Motivated by a profound conviction, you safeguard your people's hallowed traditions. As you travel to Damascus, letters in hand authorizing you to arrest followers of Jesus, something unimaginable happens. A bright light suddenly surrounds you, so intense that it brings you to your knees. You hear a voice asking, "Saul, Saul, why do you persecute me?" Confused and blinded, you ask, "Who are you, Lord?" The voice responds, "I am Jesus, whom you are persecuting" (Acts 9:3-5). This encounter with the risen Christ leaves you utterly transformed. Once a fierce opponent of the early

Church, Saul became Paul, one of its most passionate apostles.

After this life-altering encounter, Saul is led into Damascus, blinded and helpless. For three days, he neither eats nor drinks, reflecting on the profound experience that has shattered his previous convictions (Acts 9:9). Meanwhile, in the city, a disciple named Ananias receives a vision from the Lord, instructing him to visit Saul. Understandably hesitant, given Saul's notorious reputation, Ananias obeys. He lays hands on Saul, saying, "Brother Saul, the Lord—Jesus, who appeared to you on the road as you were coming here—has sent me so that you may see again and be filled with the Holy Spirit" (Acts 9:17). Immediately, something like scales falls from Saul's eyes, and he regains his sight. He is baptized and begins to eat, regaining his strength (Acts 9:18-19).

To fully grasp the significance of Paul's transformation, it's imperative to contextualize it within his time's historical and cultural backdrop. Followers of Jesus referred to as "The Way," were often met with fierce resistance, especially from the Pharisees. This group, fervently committed to Jewish traditions, perceived the emerging Christian faith as a threat to their established way of life. Saul, himself a devout Pharisee and an active participant in this opposition, spearheaded the persecution of early Christians. Yet, his remarkable conversion on the Damascus road signified more than a personal metamorphosis; it marked a seminal moment in the proliferation of Christianity. As Paul, he undertook extensive missionary journeys, founded churches, and composed letters foundational to Christian doctrine and ethics. These endeavors, birthed from his encounter with the risen Christ, profoundly impacted the Christian faith and its teachings.

The transformation from Saul, the zealous persecutor, to Paul, a cornerstone of the Church, highlights the transformative power of faith. This journey represents a crucial phase in the Christian story and provides essential theological insights and guidance through his writings in the New Testament, which remain influential in Christian thought and practice. The story of Paul's conversion offers profound lessons on personal transformation and mission. In modern times, many individuals experience life-changing moments that redefine their paths. Consider Malcolm X, who transformed from a criminal into a prominent civil rights activist after a spiritual awakening. Like Paul's, this transformation underscores the power of embracing one's calling and mission with faith and determination.

Reflecting on your own experiences, have you ever encountered a moment that transformed your faith journey? Perhaps a challenging situation led you to a deeper understanding of your purpose, or an unexpected event redirected your path. These moments of transformation are often accompanied by clarity and renewed purpose. Embracing them involves recognizing the divine call and stepping forward with courage and faith.

Consider what steps you can take to fulfill your divine mission. It might involve engaging in community service or using your talents to support others. Identifying and actively pursuing your mission can bring a profound sense of fulfillment and contribute to the greater good.

PETER'S VISION: INCLUSIVITY IN FAITH

See yourself as Peter, for whom traditions and dietary laws have long defined faith and personal identity. On a tranquil afternoon, a trance envelops you as you earnestly pray on a rooftop in Joppa. A vast sheet descends from above, filled with all kinds of animals, reptiles, and birds—species you've always considered unclean. A divine voice commands, "Rise, Peter. Kill and eat." Baffled and repulsed, you retort, "By no means, Lord! I have never eaten anything impure or unclean." Yet, the voice firmly counters, "What God has made clean, do not call impure." This intense exchange recurs three times before the vision dissipates (Acts 10:9-16).

Left in astonishment by this revelation, you're compelled to ponder its significance. At that moment, divine providence aligns with messengers from Cornelius, a Roman centurion guided by a heavenly vision, who come seeking you. Agreeing to meet Cornelius, you soon realize the profound meaning of your vision. It was never solely about dietary restrictions; it represented a divine directive to dissolve the longstanding divisions between Jews and Gentiles (Acts 10:17-20).

Arriving at Cornelius's house, Peter preaches the gospel, and as he speaks, the Holy Spirit falls upon all who are listening, including the Gentiles. They begin speaking in tongues and praising God, just as the apostles had experienced at Pentecost. Peter then asks, "Can anyone keep these people from being baptized with water? They have received the Holy Spirit just as we have" (Acts 10:44-48). This moment signifies a monumental shift in the early Church, opening the doors of faith to Gentiles without requiring them to adhere to Jewish customs.

Fully appreciating Peter's vision necessitates understanding the significance of dietary laws within Jewish culture. Recorded in Leviticus, these regulations transcended mere dietary preferences to embody principles of purity and distinction from Gentiles. Eating certain foods or associating with non-Jews could make one ceremonially unclean. This separation was deeply ingrained in Jewish culture and religion. However, as the early Church grew, debates arose about whether Gentile converts needed to follow these laws. Peter's vision and subsequent experiences played a crucial role in shaping the Church's stance on inclusivity, leading to the Jerusalem Council, where it was decided that Gentiles did not need to adopt Jewish customs to be part of the Christian community.

Peter's vision holds invaluable lessons for us today, especially regarding inclusivity and acceptance in our faith communities. Many modern faith communities strive to embrace diversity, recognizing that the kingdom of God is open to all, regardless of background, race, or social status. Examples abound of churches and religious groups working to break down barriers and welcome everyone. Whether through inclusive worship practices, community outreach programs, or fostering open dialogues about race and equality, these efforts echo the spirit of Peter's vision.

Reflect on your own experiences with inclusivity and acceptance. How do you practice these principles in your faith community? Consider moments when you might have felt excluded or, conversely, when you have extended a welcoming hand to someone different from yourself. What steps can you take to break down barriers and create a more inclusive environment? This might involve educating yourself about other cultures, actively participating in community events, or simply being open to conversations with those who have different perspectives. The story of Peter's vision reminds us that God's love knows no boundaries, and we are called to reflect that boundless love in our actions and attitudes.

THE EARLY CHURCH: COMMUNITY AND COMMITMENT

Picture the early Christian community in the bustling city of Jerusalem. These believers were not just attending occasional gatherings but building a new way of life together. Their devotion to the apostles' teaching and fellowship was evident in every aspect of their daily lives (Acts 2:42). They met regularly to learn from the apostles, discuss the teachings of Jesus, and support one another in their faith. It wasn't just about attending a weekly service but creating a vibrant, living community grounded in shared beliefs and mutual support.

Imagine walking into one of their gatherings. You would see people from all walks of life sharing their possessions to meet the needs of all members. This practice of communal living was radical, especially in a society that valued individual wealth and status. They sold their property and possessions, distributing the proceeds to needy people (Acts 2:44-45). This wasn't just charity; it was a profound expression of their commitment to one another and the teachings of Jesus. It was about living out the command to love one's neighbor in the most tangible way possible.

Meals were a central part of their fellowship. The breaking of bread in homes wasn't just about eating together; it was a sacred act of communion, a reminder of Jesus' sacrifice and their new covenant (Acts 2:46-47). These communal meals fostered deep bonds, creating a sense of family among the believers. They ate together with glad and sincere hearts, praising God and enjoying the favor of all the people. This genuine joy and unity attracted others to join their community.

It's essential to grasp the socio-economic backdrop of the first-century Mediterranean world to fully appreciate the early Christians' communal practices. Society then was deeply entrenched in systems of patronage and reciprocity, where the affluent provided for the less fortunate in return for allegiance and services. Contrary to this norm, early Christians pioneered a community of equality, where resources were shared generously among all members, irrespective of their social standing. This revolutionary form of living didn't just address material needs; it also wove a tight-knit fabric of unity and mutual support that enhanced the community's resilience and appeal to those outside its bounds.

The impact of these communal practices on the spread of Christianity cannot be overstated. The early Church's commitment to sharing resources and supporting one another created a robust, united front that could withstand external pressures and persecution. It also showcased a compelling alternative to the time's hierarchical and often exploitative social structures. The sense of belonging, purpose, and mutual care that characterized the early Christian community was a powerful draw for many people, leading to the Church's rapid growth.

Modern faith communities can draw valuable lessons from the early Church's example. Many contemporary churches and religious groups are rediscovering the importance of communal living and shared resources. For instance, some urban churches have created community gardens, where members work together to grow food shared with those in need. Others have established funds to help members facing financial hardships, ensuring that no one in the community suffers alone. These initiatives echo the early Church's commitment to mutual support and resource sharing.

Commitment to communal worship and prayer is another vital aspect of building a solid faith community. Regular gatherings for worship, prayer, and study strengthen individual faith and build a sense of unity and purpose. In a world where isolation and individualism are prevalent, the Church's role as a community of believers becomes even more crucial. By fostering a culture of mutual support, prayer, and shared learning, faith communities can offer a lifeline to those seeking connection and meaning.

Reflect on your own experiences with community and commitment. How do you contribute to the sense of community in your faith community? Perhaps you volunteer your time, offer financial support, or simply provide a listening ear to those in need. Every act of kindness and support strengthens the bonds of the community. What steps can you take to deepen your commitment to communal worship and support? Consider setting aside regular times for prayer and study with others, volunteering for community projects, or reaching out to those who may feel isolated.

The early Church's example of community and commitment challenges us to rethink how we live out our faith. It calls us to move beyond individualism and embrace a lifestyle of mutual care and support, reflecting the love and teachings of Jesus in every aspect of our lives. By doing so, we strengthen our faith communities and offer a compelling witness to what it means to follow Christ.

CONCLUSION

As we draw this exploration to a close, I hope that "An Adult Reading of Bible Stories" has reignited your faith and deepened your understanding. This book was crafted to guide adults through a thoughtful rereading of 50 Bible narratives, viewed through the lens of maturity and depth. Far from mere childhood tales, these stories are rich with insights into faith, doubt, and spiritual maturation. Whether you find yourself skeptical, distanced from your faith, or simply inquisitive, this work was designed to offer you a sanctuary for reflection, answers, and a step closer to enlightenment. Throughout the book, we delved into various stories from the Old and New Testaments. We examined the layers of meaning in these ancient texts and their relevance to our modern lives. Let's recap some of the main points we explored:

In the beginning, we revisited the Creation story and its symbolic meanings. We discussed the moral and relational likeness to God, the importance of rest, and our stewardship over creation. This set the stage for understanding human nature and redemption through the story of Adam and Eve, highlighting temptation and the need for personal accountability.

We then journeyed with the Patriarchs, from Abraham's call to trust God's promises to Sarah's laughter amidst doubt. We saw faith in action with Isaac and Rebekah's union and profound dreams in Jacob's Ladder. These stories illustrated the transformative power of faith and obedience.

Moving into the Exodus, we followed Moses' calling, Egypt's plagues, and the Red Sea's miraculous parting. These events underscored divine justice, human perseverance, and reliance on God's provision.

The Judges and their deliverance showed us the strength of Deborah's leadership, Gideon's search for divine assurance, Samson's balance of power and weakness, and Ruth's loyalty. These narratives emphasized the importance of humility, faith, and community support.

As we explored the Kings and Prophets, we learned from Samuel's listening, Saul's pride, David's courage, and Solomon's wisdom. The messages of the Major and Minor Prophets, from Isaiah's vision of hope to Malachi's promise of faithfulness, offered lessons on maintaining hope, embracing divine mercy, and standing firm in faith.

In the New Testament, we reflected on Mary's faith in the unseen, John the Baptist's call to repentance, Jesus' baptism and temptation, and the early church's community and commitment. These stories emphasized the importance of spiritual preparation, trusting in one's divine mission, and fostering a sense of community.

Key takeaways from this journey include the timeless relevance of these Bible stories. They remind us of the importance of faith, humility, accountability, and community. They teach us to trust in God's provision and to seek divine guidance in our lives.

I encourage you to continue exploring these stories and reflecting on their lessons. Whether through personal reflection, group discussions, or further reading, let these stories inspire and guide you. Take the time to practice stewardship in your community, show forgiveness, and stand firm in your beliefs.

Remember, it's okay to have questions and doubts. What matters is your willingness to seek answers and grow spiritually. As a choir member with my questions and doubts, I've found that embracing the complexity of faith has deepened my understanding and connection to the Gospel.

Thank you for joining me on this journey. May these stories continue to illuminate your path, provide comfort in times of doubt, and inspire you to live a life of faith and understanding. Keep seeking, keep reflecting, and keep growing. Your journey with the Living Word is just beginning.

REFERENCES

Sellers in Nigeria. https://www.infoisinfo.ng/search/book-seller

Deltek and SoDA Teaming Up To Host Agency Industry Event. https://kopavguldxhlgut.netlify.app/14456/63629.html

Dermatologically Tested Haircare: our well-being manifesto | Rossano Ferretti Parma. https://www.rossanoferretti.com/eu/dermatologically-tested-haircare-our-well-being-manifesto/

One Small Gesture or Encouraging Word - Omega. https://omeganw.org/one-small-gesture-or-encouraging-word/

Garden of eden meaning in Hindi - गार्डन मतलब हिंदी में - Translation. https://dict.hinkhoj.com/garden%20of%20eden-meaning-in-hindi.words

Symbolism of 'Tree of Knowledge of Good and Evil' in Different Religions - Spiritual Ray. https://spiritualray.com/symbolism-of-tree-of-knowledge-of-good-evil-in-different-religions

Why Did Adam And Eve Eat The Apple? https://nwaonline.org/why-did-adam-and-eve-eat-the-apple/

Baby's Out of Luck Again by April June - Independent Music Reviews. https://independentmusic.reviews/babys-out-of-luck-again-by-april-june/

10 Thought-Provoking Tuesdays With Morrie Journal Prompts To Inspire Self-Reflection - Coloringfolder.com. https://coloringfolder.com/tuesdays-with-morrie-journal-prompts/

How Many Archangels Are There in Catholicism | Christian.net. https://christian.net/theology-and-spirituality/how-many-archangels-are-there-in-catholicism/

awsansc01exam | Trinacria Cultura. https://www.trinacriaciclismo.com/forum/benvenuto-nel-forum/awsansc01exam/dl-486755f5-36d1-4c50-8b18-a942379167a7

Genesis 15:5 - He took him outside and said, "Look up at the sky and count the stars—if indeed you can count them." Then he said to him, "So shall your offspring be.". https://genesis.bible/genesis-15-5/

The Power Of Reading And Meditating On The Bible | ShunSpirit. https://shunspirit.com/article/do-people-read-and-meditate-on-thebible

Insider's Guide: GDP - Deleted Scene - E355 Revealed. https://www.tipstrendy.com/gdp-deleted-scene-e355/

Why Take Courses at Noahide Academy? 1. Expertise and Auth | Noahide Fellowship | Noahide Academy. https://www.noahideacademy.org/group/noahide-fellowship/discussion/8141fe85-a350-470b-98e2-623d5aeaf541

Warbler's spiritual meaning. https://spiritualrealm.org/warbler-spiritual-meaning/

Exodus 3:11 ESV - But Moses said to God, "Who am... | Biblia. https://biblia.com/bible/esv/exodus/3/11

Custody: Can a grandparent get visitation? | WomensLaw.org. https://www.womenslaw.org/laws/me/custody/who-can-get-parental-rights-and-responsibilities-andor-visitation/can-grandparent

Surin, K. (2023). The American Politics of French Theory: Derrida, Deleuze, Guattari, and Foucault in Translation by Jason Demers (review). SubStance. https://doi.org/10.1353/sub.2023.a907154

Consecration of the Firstborn; Crossing the Sea – Dave R Phillips. https://daverphillips.com/consecration-of-the-firstborn-crossing-the-sea/

Guevara, R. C. O. (2020). On Journeys and Crossroads. https://core.ac.uk/download/335034187.pdf

Luke in the Land. https://btcreidsville.com/luke-in-the-land

Why Do We Observe Sunday as the Sabbath Day? - The Remnant Church of Jesus Christ of Latter-Day Saints. https://theremnantchurch.com/why-do-we-observe-sunday-as-the-sabbath-day/

What do you praise God for? - My Step with God - The Uncommon Pursuit Community. https://up.uncommonpursuit.net/t/what-do-you-praise-god-for/4781

Chosen by God: An Invitation to Unite All to Christ - Mountain City Church. https://mountaincity.church/2023/07/chosen-by-god-an-invitation-to-unite-all-to-christ/

Fleet, D. (2021). Fuel and faith: A spiritual geography of fossil fuels in Western Canada. https://core.ac.uk/download/481573910.pdf

Majule, G. P. (2012). Salt and light: Best ministry practices for community impact by Tanzanian churches. https://core.ac.uk/download/155817813.pdf

Numbers 21:5 spoke against God and against Moses: "Why have you led us up out of Egypt to die in the wilderness? There is no bread or water, and we detest this wretched food!". https://mail.biblehub.com/numbers/21-5.htm

Message - The serpent of brass: everyone who will look at it, shall live. https://the-new-way.org/messages/the_serpent_of_brass.....html

God's Irony: Death Symbolizes Life - by Jane Korvemaker. https://www.missiodeicatholic.org/p/gods-irony-death-symbolizes-life

Numbers 21:8 - The LORD said to Moses, "Make a snake and put it u.... https://www.biblestudytools.com/numbers/21-8.html.

Tree of Life – PLICC. https://plicc.org/the-tree-of-life/

Pena, N. (2019). Engineering the Rod of Asclepius – A Biochemical Investigation of Snake Venom Components and their Application as Potential Cancer Treatments. https://core.ac.uk/download/213463828.pdf

What do you praise God for? - My Step with God - The Uncommon Pursuit Community. https://up.uncommonpursuit.net/t/what-do-you-praise-god-for/4781

Chosen by God: An Invitation to Unite All to Christ - Mountain City Church. https://mountaincity.church/2023/07/chosen-by-god-an-invitation-to-unite-all-to-christ/

Fleet, D. (2021). Fuel and faith: A spiritual geography of fossil fuels in Western Canada. https://core.ac.uk/download/481573910.pdf

Majule, G. P. (2012). Salt and light: Best ministry practices for community impact by Tanzanian churches. https://core.ac.uk/download/155817813.pdf

Message - The serpent of brass: everyone who will look at it, shall live. https://the-new-way.org/messages/the_serpent_of_brass.....html

God's Irony: Death Symbolizes Life - by Jane Korvemaker. https://www.missiodeicatholic.org/p/gods-irony-death-symbolizes-life

Numbers 21:8 - The LORD said to Moses, "Make a snake and put it u.... https://www.biblestudytools.com/numbers/21-8.html.

Pena, N. (2019). Engineering the Rod of Asclepius – A Biochemical Investigation of Snake Venom Components and their Application as Potential Cancer Treatments. https://core.ac.uk/download/213463828.pdf

Cultural Beauty Standards: A Global Perspective. https://dailyswine.com/cultural-beauty-standards-a-global-perspective/

What Is The History Of Knoxville, TN? | Emergency Dentist of Knoxville. https://emergencydentistofknoxville.com/what-is-the-history-of-knoxville-tn/

The Trumpet Call. https://gracecity.buzzsprout.com/569593/10699069

strength for the weak – Tell Me the Story. https://talkingwithjesusblog.wordpress.com/tag/strength-for-the-weak/

Our End-of-Season Review Process. https://www.vegetableacademy.com/post/our-end-of-season-review-process

Meringolo, D. D. (2022). Radical Roots. https://doi.org/10.3998/mpub.12366495

Eros Conjunct Juno: Igniting Passion and Soul Connections. https://astromatrix.org/Horoscopes/Planet-Aspects/Eros-Conjunct-Juno

(2016). The Progression of Separation: Genesis 13 in the Hebrew Bible and Early Reception. https://core.ac.uk/download/42123055.pdf

Zechariah 007 – The City of God's Habitation - Sugar Land Bible Church | slbc.org. https://slbc.org/sermon/zechariah-007-the-city-of-gods-habitation/

Shadow Work Guide: Unveiling the Depths of Self-Exploration.https://rediscoveringsacredness.com/a-comprehensive-shadow-work-guide-unveiling-the-depths-of-self-exploration/

5 Lessons From the Life of Obadiah. https://www.thenewman.org.ng/2024/01/5-lessons-from-life-of-obadiah.html

Guenter, K. (2019). The Word Of The Lord To The Ruling Houses In Samuel And Kings. Journal of the Evangelical Theological Society, 62(2), 307-327.

Verse Of Monday, June 24, 2024 [1 Samuel 15:23] (All Versions) - Free-biblestudyhub.com. https://www.freebiblestudyhub.com/archives/7969

Verse Of Monday, June 24, 2024 [1 Samuel 15:23] (All Versions) - Free-biblestudyhub.com. https://www.freebiblestudyhub.com/archives/7969

Pierce, G. A. (1996). Evangelical Visitor - January, 1996 Vol. 109. No. 1. https://core.ac.uk/download/337615895.pdf

Yap, T. (2022). The Function Of The Women's Victory Song In 1 Samuel. Journal of the Evangelical Theological Society, 65(2), 277-288.

Forrest, B. K. (1984). Exploring Bible History. https://digitalcommons.georgefox.edu/cgi/viewcontent.cgi?article=1266&context=wes_theses

Archives | The Edge Media Philippines. https://edgemedia.ph/2023/12/19/

Tabernacle. https://thetwelvetribesofisrael.com/tabernacle

Shadow Work Guide: Unveiling the Depths of Self-Exploration.https://rediscoveringsacredness.com/a-comprehensive-shadow-work-guide-unveiling-the-depths-of-self-exploration/

While We're Waiting - Rejoice. https://rejoiceministries.org/while-were-waiting-2/

Elijah and Elisha: A Captivating Tale of Biblical Mentorship | Ancient Bible. https://ancient.biz/blog/elijah-and-elisha-a-captivating-tale-of-biblical-mentorship

Let none escape – Grace in Waves. https://graceinwaves.com/2019/07/17/let-none-escape/

Devotional Blog 11 | WMC Youth and Young Adults. https://youth.worldmethodistcouncil.org/2013/06/10/devotional-blog-11/

Lebeuf, A. (2012). What does the Bible tell us about Megaliths? https://core.ac.uk/download/229248118.pdf

Charles Grandison Finney | The Ministry of Harry Kilbride. https://kilbrideministries.com/revival/charles-grandison-finney/

1 Kings 18:36-37 At the time of sacrifice, the prophet Elijah stepped forward and prayed: "LORD, the God of Abraham, Isaac, and Israel, let it be known today that you are God in Israel and that I am your servant and ha | New International Version (NIV) | Download The Bible App Now. https://www.bible.com/bible/111/1KI.18.36-37

Thoughts from the Well: Throw another Bucket on the Bonfire.https://www.burdinefamily.com/2011/05/throw-another-bucket-on-bonfire.html

Reflections of a Demonologist - Demonologist Stephen Bridges Jr.. https://www.the-demonologist.com/8203reflections-of-a-demonologist-the-1-demonology-blog-in-the-world/baal-worshipthe-demonic-origins-of-cutting-and-slashing-of-skin

In Order to Act in Faith We Must First Act in Obedience to God's Word! - Belhaven Free Methodist Church. https://belhavenchurch.ca/in-order-to-act-in-faith-we-must-first-act-in-obedience-to-gods-word/

Divine Help in the Bible: 10 Examples Explored. https://scripturalthinking.com/examples-of-divine-help-in-the-bible/

Living Out Faith Through Actions - Day 1 | Community Life Church. https://clifec.com/living-out-faith-through-actions-day-1/

Our End-of-Season Review Process. https://www.vegetableacademy.com/post/our-end-of-season-review-process

Suffering and Deliverance (Part 32) - Daniel | The Excelsior Springs Church. https://kjvchurch.com/suffering-and-deliverance-32/

How many lions were in the den with Daniel? https://marquetapage.be/2m568fen/how-many-lions-were-in-the-den-with-daniel

The origins of Yahweh – "Religion Is The Disease – Research Is The Cure". https://tgpretender.co.uk/2719-2/

A Word from the Vine No. 345: Equipped for Battle: 5 Christian Weapons for You to Use Against The World. https://www.danishcountrysidechapel.org/post/a-word-from-the-vine-no-345-equipped-for-battle-5-christian-weapons-for-you-to-use-against-the-world

Psalm 23 nrsv. http://franchising-und-cooperation.de/archive/psalm-23-nrsv-8f2c63

Psalms Series Group Curriculum - Twin Lakes Baptist Church. https://twinlakesbaptist.com/resources/all/psalms-series-curriculum

The Meaning Behind Dreams About Your Girlfriend Cheating on You: A Comprehensive Interpretation. https://dreamynavigator.com/dream-about-girlfriend-cheating-on-me/

Our Authors - Joyce Ritchie - Author Academy Elite. https://authoracademyelite.com/our-authors-joyce-ritchie

50 Bible Verses about Losing Friends – Verse And Prayers. https://versesandprayers.com/bible-verses-about-losing-friends/

Ecclesiastes 1:2 NIV - "Meaningless!… | Biblia. https://biblia.com/bible/niv/ecclesiastes/1/2

Gilbert, B. D. (2012). The Horizon of Happiness. https://core.ac.uk/download/303944168.pdf

Ecclesiastes 3:1-8 For everything there is a season, and a time for every matter under heaven: a time to be born, and a time to die; a time to plant, and a time to pluck up what is planted; a time to kill, and a time t | English Standard Version 2016 (ESV) | Download The Bible App Now. https://www.bible.com/bible/59/ecc.3.1-8.esv

'Memento Mori Ergo Carpe Diem' - by Alejandro Betancourt. https://abetancourt.substack.com/p/memento-mori-ergo-carpe-diem

(2014). A Christmas Message from the Clergy. Consort Enterprise, (), A.21.

65 17-19. https://forsaljningavaktieraxcn.web.app/58397/367.html

February 18, 2022 – Central Union Church. https://centralunionchurch.org/february-18-2022/

Crasta, V. (2020). "By His Wounds We Are Healed:" Meditation on the Five Wounds of Jesus. https://doi.org/10.5281/zenodo.4064531

(2013). A Call to Political and Social Activism: The Jeremiadic Discourse of Maria Miller Stewart, 1831-1833. https://core.ac.uk/download/48828722.pdf

Jeremiah 20:7-9 You deceived me, LORD, and I was deceived; you overpowered me and prevailed. I am ridiculed all day long; everyone mocks me. Whenever I speak, I cry out proclaiming violence and destruction. So the wo | New International Version (NIV) | Download The Bible App Now. https://www.bible.com/bible/111/jer.20.7-9

Haas, S. (2014). Charles Blow talks truth in 'Fire Shut Up In My Bones'. The Boston Banner, 50(10), 2.

Decoding the Vision of the Valley of Dry Bones in Ezekiel Chapter 37 - Reference.com. https://www.reference.com/world-view/decoding-vision-valley-dry-bones-ezekiel-chapter

The Complete Idiot's Guide to World Religions (2nd Edition) - SILO.PUB. https://silo.pub/the-complete-idiots-guide-to-world-religions-2nd-edition.html

Weekly Devotion for March 13, 2023 - Wisconsin Conference of the UMC. https://www.wisconsinumc.org/post/weekly-devotion-for-march-13-2023-17341383

Nine of Pentacles Explained - Upright & Reversed Meanings. https://backyardbanshee.com/tarot/card-meanings/minor-arcana/nine-of-pentacles-coins-disks/

(2021). A verse for today. Florida Times Union, (), A-8.

Introduction to Volume 18 - Milken Archive of Jewish Music. https://www.milkenarchive.org/articles/view/introduction-to-volume-18

News – Tagged "grief" – The Workout Witch. https://theworkoutwitch.com/blogs/news/tagged/grief

(2006). Struggle in the ethics of technology. Koers - Bulletin for Christian Scholarship. https://doi.org/10.4102/koers.v71i1.235

Grassroots Movements for Equal Utility Access in Immigrant Communities in Minnesota – USCIS Guide. https://www.uscisguide.com/living/grassroots-movements-for-equal-utility-access-in-immigrant-communities-in-minnesota/

Exploring the Teachings of Jesus in the New Testament | Famous Gold State. https://famousgoldstate.com/30548-exploring-the-teachings-of-jesus-in-the-new-testament-06/

Prayer For Justice For The Poor And Helpless. https://imotivatecameroon.com/prayer-for-justice-for-the-poor-and-helpless/

Sanctuary: Prayers for a New Home or Apartment | Christian Pure. https://www.christianpure.com/learn/new-home-apartment-prayers

Step 2 of NA: Unearthing Strength & Building Hope. https://advancedaddictioncenter.com/addiction-recovery/step-2-of-na/

Malachi 1:8 When you offer blind animals for sacrifice, is that not wrong? When you sacrifice lame or diseased animals, is that not wrong? Try offering them to your governor! Would he be pleased with you? Would he accept you?" says the LORD Almighty.. https://bibleapps.com/malachi/1-8.htm

Museum Huertgen Forest 1944 and in Peacetime. https://www.europeremembers.com/pois/231/museum-huertgen-forest-1944-and-in-peacetime

What Does The Water Symbolize In Baptism? | Christian.net https://christian.net/theology-and-spirituality/what-does-the-water-symbolize-in-baptism/

References 11

Dane Davis: Christmas at the Movies: The Nativity Story. https://blog.greaterimpact.cc/2016/12/christmas-at-movies-nativity-story.html

Levitsky, A. A. (2018). The Song from the Singer: Personification, Embodiment, and Anthropomorphization in Troubadour Lyric. https://doi.org/10.7916/D80G52JR

Romans 12 Biblical Illustrator. https://mail.biblehub.com/commentaries/illustrator/romans/12.htm

Stepp, A. (2014). Shifting to a Missional Culture at First Presbyterian Church of Houston. https://core.ac.uk/download/230647813.pdf

Luke 3:4 NIV: As it is written in the book of the words of Isaiah the prophet: "A voice of one calling in the wilderness, 'Prepare the way for the Lord, make straight paths for him.. https://www.biblehub.com/niv/luke/3-4.htm

2023 December 16. https://www.thestoryandyou.com/2023/12/16/

John The Baptist and Mrs. Nolan / Second Sunday in Advent – Bethel Lutheran Church. https://www.bethelwillowick.org/john-the-baptist-and-mrs-nolan-second-sunday-in-advent/

Saint Paul's Journey Inspires Personal Change. http://allagesofgeek.com/saint-pauls-journey-inspires-personal-change/

Pentecost Sunday Prayer Celebrating the Gift of the Holy Spirit - Prayer Ideas. https://www.prayerideas.org/pentecost-sunday-prayer-celebrating-the-gift-of-the-holy-spirit/

First Time Love Is Mentioned in the Bible [BiblePeople]. https://www.bible-people.info/first-time-love-is-mentioned-in-the-bible/

2020 March. https://brisbanehebrewcongregation.com/2020/03/

Why Abraham is Called the Father of Faith - JESUSCANDOIT. https://jesuscandoit.com/why-abraham-is-called-the-father-of-faith/

Paying Attention – David Freitag. https://davidpatrickfreitag.com/2023/01/07/paying-attention/

Covaciu, C. (2020). The Bread of Life. LAP LAMBERT Academic Publishing EBooks. https://www.knigozal.com/store/ru/book/the-bread-of-life/isbn/978-620-0-53962-5

MATTHEW 04:01-11 JESUS OVERCOMES TEMPTATION | Bible interpretation by Fr. Abraham Mutholath. https://bibleinterpretation.org/matthew-4_1-11/

Matthew 4:7 NLT - Jesus responded, "The… | Biblia. https://biblia.com/bible/nlt/matthew/4/7

How Can Our High Priest Empathize with Us? (Hebrews 4:15). https://www.christianity.com/wiki/jesus-christ/how-can-our-high-priest-empathize-with-us.html

Harris, G. (2006). Teaching Through a Mirror Dimly: Partnering with Christ to Overcome Self. https://digitalcommons.georgefox.edu/cgi/viewcontent.cgi?article=1013&context=icctej

Promised land – SELENA BOYTS. https://selenaboyts.com/tag/promised-land/

Every adversity, every failure, every heartbreak, carries with it the seed of an equal or greater benefit.. https://elevatesociety.com/every-adversity-every-failure-every/

Building a Strong MVP Brand: Strategies and Best Practices for MVP Branding.   https://dotndot.com/building-a-strong-mvp-brand-strategies-and-best-practices-for-mvp-branding/

Strawberry Cookie Wiki | XLA Multiverse. https://x.la/multiverse/universes/cookie-run-kingdom/characters/strawberry-cookie-characterpage

Ananias Biblical Meaning - Dreamophile. https://dreamophile.com/biblical-meanings/ananias-biblical-meaning/

Acts 9:17 NASB95 - So Ananias departed and… | Biblia. https://biblia.com/bible/nasb95/acts/9/17

Rivas, H., Long, B., Resner, A., White, E. F., Neller, K. V., Jackson, D., Willis, J. T., York, J., Tate, W., & Woodroof, J. (1991). 1991: Abilene Christian College Bible Lectures - Full Text. https://core.ac.uk/download/55326034.pdf

24 | April | 2016 | Grace Episcopal Church (Sheldon, VT). https://gracechurchsheldon.com/2016/04/24/

Acts 10:47 KJV 1900 - Can any man forbid water,… | Biblia. https://biblia.com/bible/kjv1900/acts/10/47

What is the difference between Jews and Gentiles? https://biblechat.ai/knowledgebase/new-testament/pauline-epistles/what-difference-between-jews-gentiles/

Exploring the Bible Definition of Fellowship: A Deep Dive - Biblical Definitions. https://biblicaldefinitions.com/bible-definition-of-fellowship/

Foster, A. L. (2019). Declining Inner-City Church Membership: Creating Spiritually Healthy Inner-City Churches through Acts 2:42-47. https://core.ac.uk/download/213463503.pdf

Foster, A. L. (2019). Declining Inner-City Church Membership: Creating Spiritually Healthy Inner-City Churches through Acts 2:42-47. https://core.ac.uk/download/213463503.pdf